Skyhorse Publishing books may be purchased in bulk at special discounts for sales promotion, corporate gifts, fund-raising, or educational purposes. Special editions can also be created to specifications. For details, contact the Special Sales Department, Skyhorse Publishing, 307 West 36th Street, 11th Floor, New York, NY 10018 or info@skyhorsepublishing.com.

Visit our website at www.skyhorsepublishing.com.

10 9 8 7 6 5 4 3 2 1

Library of Congress Control Number: 2023901323

Design by Noora Cox
Cover photograph by Deanna Huey
Interior photographs by Deanna Huey
Edited by Monica Sweeney

Illustrations used under license by Shutterstock.com
Print ISBN: 978-1-5107-7527-5 (paper over board)
eBook ISBN: 978-1-5107-7665-4

Printed in China

Preface

GROWING UP AND SPENDING TIME WITH MY GRANDMOTHER, I remember the many stories she would tell my siblings and me about the lantern witch that ate misbehaving children around the village. I remember her describing her long stringy black hair, sharp dirty nails, and distinctive shrill laugh. This was actually just a ploy to frighten disobedient children to behave. Even as I grew up knowing the story was untrue, I still can't help but think of my grandmother's witch stories when I see someone with long black hair or hear a sharp cackle when someone laughs.

When I was approached with the opportunity to put together *The Witch's Cookbook*, memories of sitting in my grandmother's living room watching reruns of *Bewitched* together and growing up obsessed with the Harry Potter series came to mind. To have the opportunity to create recipes from stories I love or from ones that once frightened me wasn't something I could pass up. Better yet, this was a chance to delve into new stories I have yet to discover.

The depictions of witches vary in the collection of stories by which these recipes are inspired. The modern-day witches we see in *The Vampire Diaries* and *Charmed* are contemporary and often relatable. It's quite a contrast when we think about the witches we see in *Hocus Pocus* and *Wicked* with their big black pointy hats and cloaks. Regardless of the story or portrayal of witches we are being told, the common thread connecting them is that they're all forces of nature. Headstrong, unbending, and powerful, they are the most wonderfully complex characters in the most fascinating and beautiful ways.

Through this cookbook, you'll conjure the most delectable and memorable recipes right from the sacred kitchen of your own home. In the first chapter, you'll find wickedly delicious breakfasts to start your day and work into the next section with smaller plates and bites to fill you until dinner. Later, you'll find dishes large enough to feed a coven of any size. Finally, finish the day off with a decadent dessert and drink. Most recipes are flexible for you to use what you have on hand or with whatever herbs and vegetables may be growing in your garden.

Together we will sail to Circe's island of Aiaia, board a train to Hogwarts, and explore the wilderness of Northern Russia with Vasya. With many more amazing stories to explore in between, we uncover and learn each witchy character through the experience of cooking, eating, and sharing the stories that accompany them. Recreate the recipes that capture the spirit of our favorite magical tales that filled our books and flew across our screens.

Deanna Huey

Contents

Bewitching Breakfasts and Beginnings

Snacks, Starters, and Séances

Enticing Entrées and Enchantments

Desserts, Delights, and Divinations

Beldam Brews and Beverages

The Witches Primer

A Discovery of Witches—
All Souls Trilogy

In a narrative set in the historic city of Oxford, we follow the journey of Diana Bishop, a professor from Yale and born from a lineage of powerful witches. Her attempt to reject magic and lead a normal life starts to unravel when she opens *Ashmole 782*, the Book of Life. Vampires, witches, and daemons begin to hunt down the once lost manuscript and for any information she may have learned. One of those creatures is Matthew Clairmont, a scientist who has spent years trying to find the missing manuscript. The trilogy follows their relationship and the difficult journey of Diana discovering her powers and family history and becoming a powerful weaver. *Recipes on pages 3, 15, 117, 133, and 135.*

Bewitched

From the outside, Samantha and Darrin may seem like any ordinary couple. But Samantha reveals quite the secret to Darrin when on their honeymoon: Samantha is a witch. Darrin is completely shocked by the news, but they both agree to lead a magic-free life together. But Samantha experiences everyday struggles and funny hijinks that could so *easily* be fixed with a twitch of her nose. Not to be outdone or forgotten, Samantha's mother, Endora, often pops in to interfere, and baby Tabitha can't always control her own magical gifts. Though mischief is always brewing, Samantha and Darrin's good nature and love for one another always sparkle.
Recipes on pages 41, 77, and 87.

Brave

Set in the breathtaking landscape of the Scottish Highlands, Princess Merida of Clan DunBroch celebrates her sixteenth birthday in the medieval halls of Castle DunBroch. Independent, headstrong, and adventurous, Merida is the opposite of what her family needs if they hope to be successful in finding a worthwhile suitor. Unwilling to comply with her parents, Merida runs away and is led to a cottage owned by a woodcarving witch. The witch wouldn't be a witch if she didn't have a trick up her sleeve. The witch convinces Merida to buy her entire collection of wooden creations in return for a spell to change her fate. *Recipe on page 121.*

Buffy the Vampire Slayer

Blonde, beautiful, and born in the sunshine of Los Angeles, Buffy Summers is an unlikely superhero. At just fifteen years old, she is called on as "the Chosen One." Her destiny as a vampire slayer sometimes feels like a curse, but Buffy is no ordinary slayer and fights to take down every "Big Bad" that comes her way. With the help of the Scooby Gang and circle of allies, they often battle these evil forces with their own strengths in witchcraft, supernatural abilities, and knowledge. Buffy is girl power incarnate: she fights evil all while trying to survive high school.
Recipes on pages 11, 67, 101, and 107.

Charmed

The Halliwell sisters, Prue, Piper, and Phoebe, thought they had a fairly normal upbringing, but all that changes when Phoebe returns to her childhood home and stumbles upon a spell book in the attic. Assuming it's merely decorative, Phoebe recites a spell and unknowingly activates the magic that can only work if the estranged sisters reunite. The sisters discover their powers of witchcraft to become the Power of Three, the strongest force of good witches who have the power to fight evil. Newly minted with their powers and resolved to protect and save innocents, they pay the price of such great responsibility at the cost of a sister's life. While grieving, the sisters discover the existence of a half sister, Paige, to bring back the Power of Three. *Charmed* again, the sisters fight demons and warlocks while trying to balance love, careers, and living a normal life. *Recipes on pages 13, 27, 39, 45, 75, 81, 103, and 123.*

Chilling Adventures of Sabrina

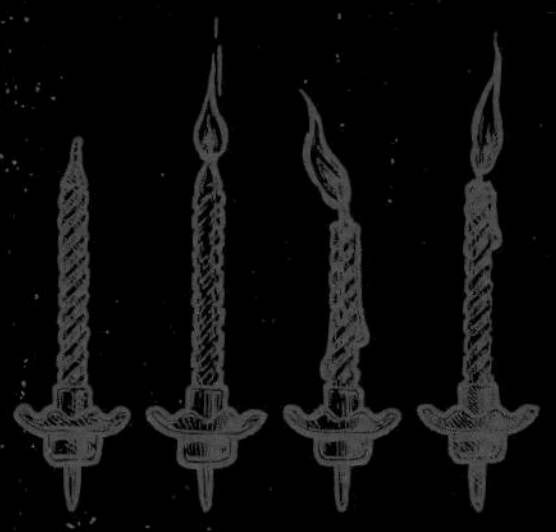

Based on the Archie comic books, *Chilling Adventures of Sabrina* debuts as the young witch prepares to celebrate her sixteenth birthday. Born as a half witch, Sabrina is an orphan who is being raised by her witchy aunts Hilda and Zelda. Having grown up close to her human friends, Sabrina now faces a difficult decision to choose between two worlds, her life as a witch or her mortal life. Faced with the threat that put her friends and family's lives at risk, Sabrina is manipulated into signing the Book of the Beast and in exchange is granted more power in order to defeat the Greendale Thirteen and the Red Angel of Death. As a half witch and half human, Sabrina is symbolic of the union between the witches and mortals. Equipped with her abilities to heal and summon hellfire, Sabrina has the magic to defeat enemies that pose any threat to her coven and the world. *Recipes on pages 17, 83, 99, 125, 139, and 151.*

Circe

In 2018, Madeline Miller released her book that breathed new life into the enthralling mythological sorceress Circe. The daughter of Helios and Perse, Circe grows up as a lonely goddess, rejected by her family who thought of her as weak and odd. Circe's powers truly emerge when she is banished from her home for dabbling with her powers and tinkering with herbs and potions. Exiled on the island of Aiaia, Circe immerses herself in her witchcraft by transforming men into swine and creating a host of lions and wolves by her side. Her difficult journey evolves into one of the most powerful and captivating stories in Greek mythology. *Recipes on pages 37 and 71.*

Enchanted

The story of *Enchanted* begins as a classic animated fairy tale of Princess Giselle, from the kingdom of Andalasia. She is set to marry and live happily ever after with the handsome Prince Edward, but the prince's mother, Queen Narissa, has other plans. Disguised as an old hag, the evil queen pushes Giselle down a well that transports her right out of the animated fairy tale and into the middle of real-life New York City. Giselle is lost but optimistic, and we follow her story as she tries to make her way back home to her prince—only to find that her original plans may not be what her heart truly desires. Queen Narissa and her enlisted servant conspire against Giselle to poison her with three poison apples in the hopes of destroying any chance of her marrying the prince. *Recipes on pages 109 and 147.*

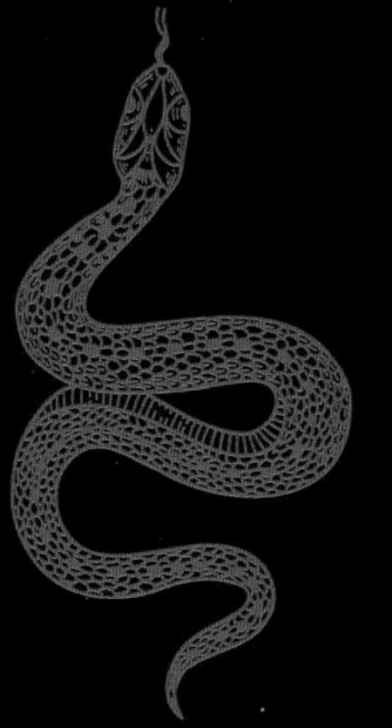

Fantastic Beasts and Where to Find Them

Set in the wizarding world of Harry Potter seventy years before the arrival of "the boy who lived," *Fantastic Beasts and Where to Find Them* follows a different batch of witches and wizards. Newt Scamander was known for his passion and talent with magical creatures throughout his years at Hogwarts School of Witchcraft and Wizardry, but this "magizoologist" might be biting off more than he can chew when he arrives in 1926 New York City. In the hustles of the busy American city, Newt's creatures escape from his magical suitcase, all thanks to a mix-up at the bank with a no-maj, Jacob Kowalski. Now with magical creatures on the loose, Newt joins Jacob, Tina, Queenie, and a host of witches and wizards on this new journey to recapture these escaped magical creatures. *Recipe on page 111.*

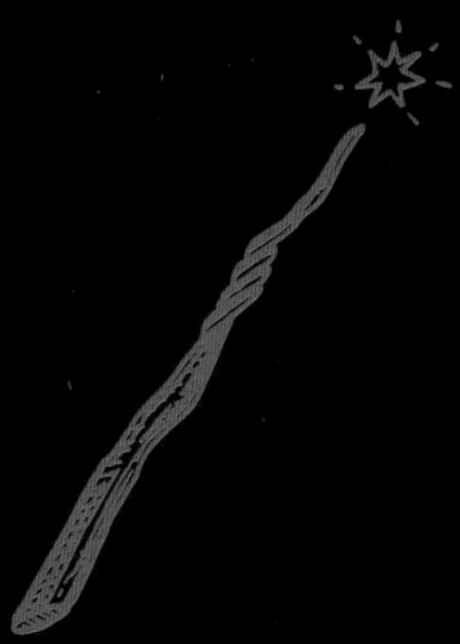

Harry Potter

Harry grew up in the disgruntled household of the Durlseys, the worst kind of Muggles. Unaware and hidden from the wizarding world from which he was born, Harry discovers on his eleventh birthday that he is actually a wizard and that his parents were murdered by the evil Lord Voldemort. With his supplies and few personal belongings, Harry is swept off to Hogwarts School of Witchcraft and Wizardry. After befriending the young witch, Hermione, she quickly becomes a lifeline for Harry and Ron as they seem to always have a knack for running into trouble. Resourceful, book smart, and loyal to the very end, Hermione always fights for her friends and for what is right. While this seven-book journey is centered around "the boy who lived," the witches in Harry's life, including Professor McGonagall, Ginny, and Hermione, are powerful and resilient in clearing the path to help Harry uncover the story of his past and bring down Lord Voldemort and all those who serve him. *Recipes on pages 89, 113, 127, 131, 143, and 145.*

Hocus Pocus

Gather around, sisters! It's been three hundred years since the Sanderson sisters, Winifred, Mary, and Sarah, were executed and cast a curse promising their vengeful return to Salem, Massachusetts. On a full moon on All Hallow's Eve, a group of foolish teenagers light the black flame candle—the key to resurrecting the witches back to modern day Salem. Now Max, Alison, and Dani must keep The Manual of Witchcraft and Alchemy safely out of the witches' hands before they can obtain the Life Potion to become immortal and wreak havoc on the children of Salem. *Recipes on pages 141 and 153.*

Howl's Moving Castle

In *Howl's Moving Castle*, the Witch of the Waste enters a hat shop in search of a girl named Sophie. Having seen her and the magician, Howl, together the night before, she becomes angry at Howl's interest in Sophie. Spiteful of Howl's turn of affection when he realizes the truth of the witch's appearance, the witch now wants Howl's heart for what he has done. Entering the shop, the witch curses Sophie to appear as a ninety-year-old hag. Horrified, she runs away in search for a cure for the curse the witch had cast upon her. As our story with the witch progresses, she is ultimately stripped of her powers, returning her to her original self, old and no longer able to care for herself. *Recipe on page 5.*

Kiki's Delivery Service

A thirteen-year-old witch, Kiki, and her cat, Jiji, traveled together from their family home to the city of Koriko. It was custom to spend a year on her own to gain independence and develop into her own as she enters adulthood. Kiki experiences her ups and downs in this new city all alone. Her extreme self-doubt and insecurities cause her to lose her magic and flying abilities. Little does she know, her powers were never really lost to begin with. All she needs is to find the courage and confidence within herself. *Recipe on page 91.*

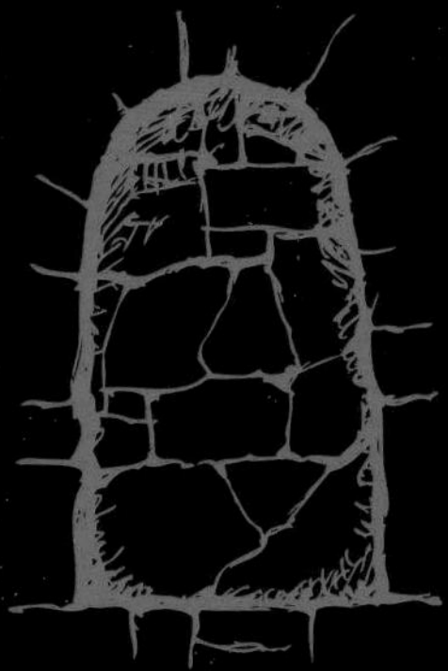

Outlander

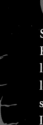

Set to celebrate their second honeymoon in the Scottish Highlands, Claire and Frank Randall arrive in Inverness ready to immerse themselves in the history and beauty of the land. After learning of a circle of standing stones nearby, Claire takes Frank to see the location when they come upon a group of women dancing and chanting to call down the sun. Claire returns back on her own the next day to suddenly hear a humming sound. Inexplicably drawn to the area, Claire touches the stone and finds herself mysteriously thrown back in time to 1743 Scotland. Trying to survive and make sense of what has happened, Claire finds herself in the hands of Clan MacKenzie and is forced to marry Jamie MacTavish for her own safety. Along the way, Claire meets Geillis Duncan, who is skilled in herbs, dark magic, and an odd interest in killing her husbands. Claire discovers Geillis is actually from the future, just like her. *Recipes on pages 29 and 55.*

Practical Magic

After learning of the family curse that those who fall in love with an Owens woman will all die an untimely death, Sally Owens makes a vow that she would never fall in love. Sally casts a spell for a man with traits so rare it would be impossible for him to be real. Her sister Gillian, however, is the opposite and is eager to fall in love. Growing up with their witchy aunts, the sisters have different outlooks on love and witchcraft. While one is cautious to never get hurt, the other throws caution to the wind. With the death of Sally's husband and Gillian's escape from an abusive relationship, the sisters reunite to support one another. Their lives begin to change with the arrival of Officer Hallet to investigate the disappearance of Jimmy Angelov, Gilly's abusive boyfriend. Seeming to match the description she described in the spell so long ago, Sally is reluctant to acknowledge the feelings she has for Officer Hallet. Forced to come to terms that in order to truly live her life, she must embrace her magic and allow herself to love. *Recipes on pages 31 and 149.*

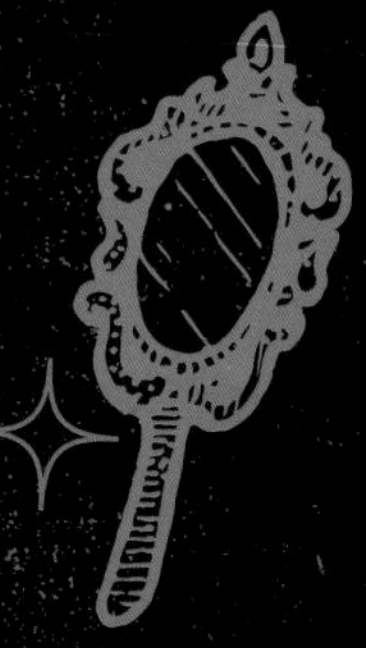

Snow White and the Seven Dwarfs

Magic mirror on the wall, who's the fairest one of all? When the magic mirror reveals that Snow White is the fairest of them all, the Evil Queen becomes furious and jealous that she was no longer considered to be the most beautiful. Obsessed and vain, the Evil Queen embarks on a mission to kill Snow White. Using witchcraft, the Evil Queen disguises herself as an old hag and conjured a poisonous apple for Snow White to eat. Just one bite will send its victim to a sleeping death. The Evil Queen will stop at nothing to reclaim herself as the most beautiful and powerful. *Recipe on page 119.*

Spirited Away

A tale about facing your fears, *Spirited Away* follows Chihiro, a ten-year-old girl on her way to move to a new town with her parents. Sidetracked with what was meant to be a quick stop on their journey, Chihiro's parents discover and gorge on a large spread of food laid out in a deserted village and are turned into pigs. A quick and sudden turn of events leads Chihiro to enter into the spirit world. Thrust into this new world, Chihiro must face her own fears to survive in order to save her parents. *Recipes on pages 19 and 51.*

Tangled

For hundreds of years, Mother Gothel had maintained her youth and beauty from a potion made out of sundrop flowers. When the flowers run out, she is desperate once again for that magical elixir. Having realized the magic has been transferred to the newly born princess named Rapunzel, Mother Gothel captures her from the castle and locks her in a tower. Rapunzel grows up knowing very little about what's beyond her tower, having been warned that the outside world is too cruel and dangerous. She spends her days reading, cooking, and, of course, brushing her very long hair. Little do they know that a charming thief would climb up the tower one day and disrupt Mother Gothel's plans. *Recipe on page 49.*

The Chronicles of Narnia

Set in Narnia during the long winter, Jadis the white witch, happens upon a boy named Edmund Pevensie. Seemingly lost in the woods and trying to avoid his imminent death, he explains to the white witch that he is the son of Adam and that his sister Lucy had entered Narnia before. Intrigued, the white witch invites him to sit next to her on the carriage for some sweets and a hot drink under the warmth of her cloak. Foolishly, Edmund complies and consumes the food and drink the witch conjures for him. Starting to feel comforted by the lure of the witch, Edmund reveals the existence of his siblings and promises to bring them to her in exchange to become prince of Narnia and more Turkish delight. This sets forth the beginning of the Golden Age Prophecy, stating that Jadis will one day be overthrown by two sons of Adam and two daughters of Eve. *Recipe on page 115.*

The Little Mermaid

Ursula, the manipulative and vicious sea witch from the depths of the ocean is our villain from the animated Disney film, *The Little Mermaid*. Easily one of the most memorable and infamous antagonists, Ursula stands true to her evil ways throughout the story. Banished from Atlantica by King Triton for her use of dark magic, our sea witch cuts a deal with his daughter, Ariel, to make her dream of becoming a human a reality. In exchange for her voice, she transforms Ariel into a human for three days. Unless Ariel receives a true love's kiss, she will belong to Ursula forever. Driven and enraged from being banished, Ursula will stop at nothing to finally get her revenge on all those who have crossed her. *Recipe on page 53.*

The Originals

The Mikaelson siblings, Klaus, Elijah, and Rebekah return to New Orleans, the city that they once dominated long ago in 1919. Klaus finds the city under the rule of Marcel, who has banned the practice of magic and kills anyone who opposes him. The French Quarter coven is forced to live under Marcel's rule as their magic is drawn from the ancestors who are buried there. Their inability to leave causes much tension and brutality between vampires and witches. With the arrival of Freya, the eldest sibling and witch of the Mikaelson family, she comes to the help of her siblings as they encounter threats to Klaus's daughter, Hope. Born as a werewolf-vampire-witch tribrid, Hope quickly becomes the target for her special lineage. Forging an alliance with the Siphoners and the nine covens of New Orleans, the Mikaelsons fight to contain the Hollow in order to protect Hope and bring peace between the siblings and the city of New Orleans. *Recipes on pages 21, 69, 79, and 137.*

The Vampire Diaries

From the outside, Mystic Falls, Virginia, looks like a fairly normal town. Take a closer look and we learn that the town actually has a long history of supernatural activity and creatures like vampires, witches, werewolves, and hybrids. Born from a long line of Salem witches, Bonnie Bennett is one of the most powerful witches we follow in the television series *The Vampire Diaries*. An incredibly loyal friend from beginning to end, Bonnie is known for her powerful witchcraft as much as her selfless acts to protect her friends. *Recipes on pages 7, 23, and 155.*

The Witches

A boy and his grandmother take a vacation together to the luxury Hotel Magnificent. Little do they know that on this vacation, the witches of Inkland are holding their annual meeting in the same hotel. After sneaking into the ballroom to train his pet mice, the boy ends up locked in the room for the meeting. The boy becomes trapped in a room full of witches with a plan to wipe out the children of England with the "Formula 86 Delayed Action Mouse-Maker" potion. Catching the scent of what could only be the smell of a child, the witches corner the boy and force the entire bottle of potion down his throat. Quick and stealthy as a newly transformed mouse, the boy escapes back to his grandmother and they devise a plan to sneak the potion into the witches' soup for dinner that evening. After a successful plan, the grandmother and boy return home to start their new and exciting adventure of wiping out the witches around the world. *Recipes on pages 43 and 47.*

Throne of Glass

Proclaimed to be the last-born witch from the Witch Kingdom, Baba Yellowlegs is a cutthroat and quick-tempered witch from the book series, *Throne of Glass* by Sarah J. Maas. As one of the Ironteeth witches, Baba Yellowlegs is an old woman with distinctive saffron-colored ankles and iron teeth. Eager for paying customers to enter her fortune-teller wagon at the carnival, Baba Yellowlegs crosses paths with the protagonist of the series, Celaena Sardonthien. Celaena sought out the witch for answers that only she might be able to provide. After a payment of gold coins for the witch to keep her secrets safe, both parties become aware that they would easily betray each other for their own interests. *Recipe on page 73.*

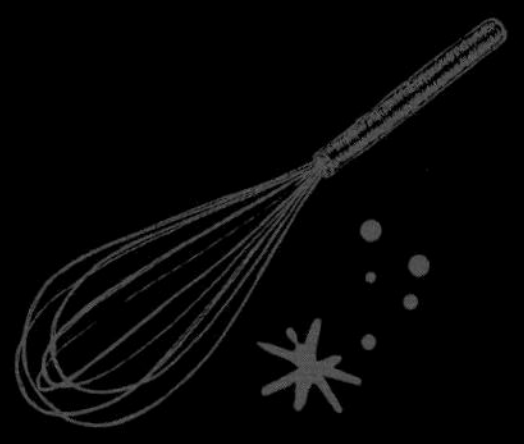

WandaVision

In the picturesque suburban neighborhood of Westview, Wanda is the charming housewife who struggles to remember the significance of the calendar day with the heart drawn on it. With the help of her neighbor Agnes, they deduce it must be an anniversary date for her and Vision. Things are not as idyllic as they seem when Vision's boss, Mr. Hart, and his wife come over for dinner. Wanda and Vision are strangely unable to answer basic questions regarding their relationship, and their dinner takes a scary turn when Mr. Hart chokes on a strawberry. After Vision removes the food from Mr. Hart's throat, their evening returns to normal and the Harts take their leave. Wanda and Vision's life continues in rapid succession as they welcome their twins, adopt a dog, and discover the odd activities happening at the outskirts of their town. Using her powers, Wanda ensures that the life she built will be protected and come to fruition exactly as she dreamed. In episodes styled after memorable sitcoms through the decades, the secrets of their neighbors and the town they live in begin to reveal themselves. *Recipes on pages 9, 59, 85, 93, 105, and 157.*

Wicked

Based on the 1995 novel by Gregory Maguire and later the wildly popular Broadway show, *Wicked*, two witches and unlikely friends, Elphaba and Glinda, meet as roommates while attending Shiz University. An outcast since the day she was born, Elphaba is often made fun of because of her emerald-green skin, her talent for magic, and her shy demeanor. Through twists and turns, *Wicked* is a rare look at how the Wicked Witch of the West from the Land of Oz came to be. *Wicked* teaches the value and importance of love, friendship, and standing up for your own beliefs even when it feels like the world is against you.
Recipe on page 159.

Winternight Trilogy

The Winternight trilogy, written by Katherine Arden, includes *The Bear and the Nightingale*, *The Girl in the Tower*, and *The Winter of the Witch*. The story follows Vasya Petrovna, a young girl from a remote village in Russia, who has an ability to see and communicate with spirits, animals, and mythical creatures. In a narrative based on Russian folklore and history, Vasya lives in a world in which her demeanor and powers are abhorred. After hearing that her stepmother plans to send her off to a convent, Vasya escapes into the forest, where she meets the frost-demon. Her journey starts here as she escapes from home and battles to save the spirit and human world.
Recipes on pages 25, 35, 57, 61, 63, and 95.

CHAPTER I

Bewitching Breakfasts and Beginnings

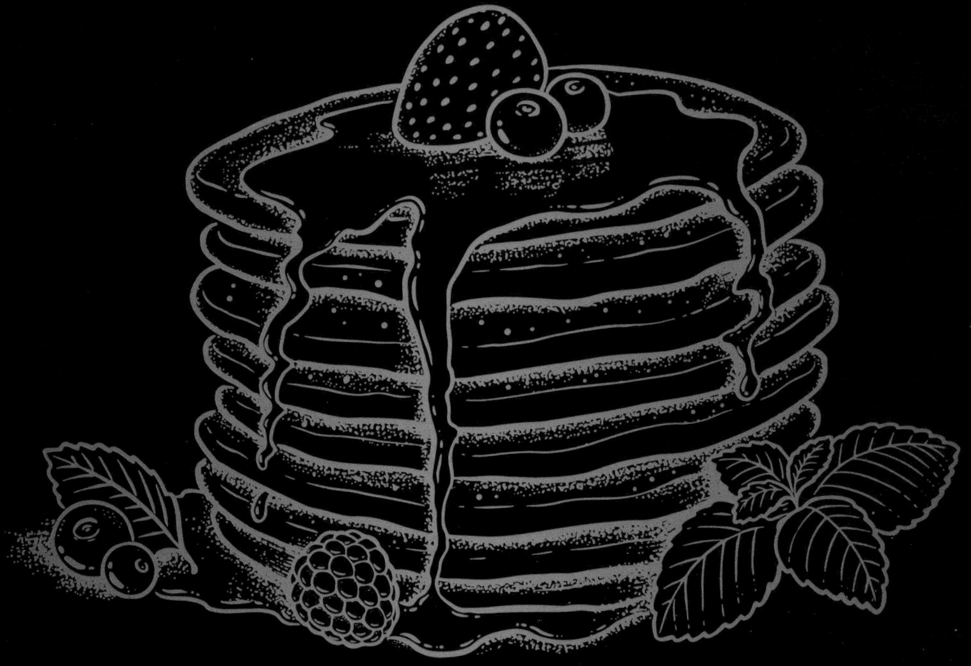

A DISCOVERY OF WITCHES:
ALL SOULS TRILOGY

MARTHE'S GOLDEN OMELET

AFTER ARRIVING AT THE CLERMONT FAMILY HOME IN FRANCE, Matthew and Marthe help Diana settle in by cooking up a golden omelet served with a large mug of tea. This omelet unveils a filling of mushrooms, cheese, and jambon de Bayonne, or cured ham, that makes the perfect breakfast for Diana to feel at home.

SERVINGS: 1–2 • PREPARATION TIME: 15 MINS • COOKING TIME: 25 MINS

INGREDIENTS

4 tablespoons unsalted butter, divided
1 shallot, minced
½ pint button mushrooms, cleaned and finely diced
½ teaspoon minced fresh thyme
salt and pepper, to taste
1 tablespoon heavy cream
3 whole eggs, beaten
⅓ cup grated Gruyère cheese
2 slices cured ham
chopped parsley, to garnish
toast, to serve

PREPARATION

1. In a skillet over medium-high heat, melt 2 tablespoons of the butter and add the minced shallot. Cook for 3 to 4 minutes, until soft.
2. Add the mushrooms and thyme. Let cook undisturbed until the liquid has evaporated. Season with salt and pepper.
3. Stir in the heavy cream and remove from the heat. Set aside to cool.
4. In a nonstick skillet over medium-low heat, melt the remaining 2 tablespoons of butter and add the beaten eggs. Season with salt and pepper.
5. Gently push and draw the cooked eggs from the edge toward the center. Once the eggs begin to set, stop stirring and gently shake the pan to redistribute the eggs evenly.
6. Sprinkle the Gruyère cheese over the eggs. Place the slices of cured ham and the mushrooms in the center. Release the edges of the omelet from the pan with a spatula. Gently fold one side over to cover the mushrooms and repeat on the other side.
7. Garnish with parsley and serve with toast.

Calcifer's Breakfast

On Sophie's first day at the castle, she and Markl prepare a great breakfast of eggs and bacon. Thick slabs of bacon are cooked over a fire until crisp and golden brown. Eggs are cracked and cooked on the side with the bacon grease, making this an indulgent and hearty way to start the day. Serve with bread, cheese, and a large bowl of tea. Just make sure to share those eggshells with Calcifer.

SERVINGS: 4 • PREPARATION TIME: 5 MINS • COOKING TIME: 15 MINS

INGREDIENTS

- 1 ¼ pounds bacon slab, sliced into four ½-inch slices
- 5 large eggs
- salt and pepper
- tea, to serve
- 1 loaf bread
- 1 wedge cheese

PREPARATION

1. Place the slices of bacon in a cast-iron pan and place over medium-high heat. When the fat starts to render and the bacon starts to crisp, flip and cook the other side. Once golden brown, pull the bacon to the side of the pan.
2. If you find there is a lot of bacon grease, drain to remove some of the fat.
3. Crack the eggs into one side of the pan (don't forget to feed Calcifer the eggshells). Lower the heat to medium and gently cook until the whites are set. Season the eggs with salt and pepper.
4. Serve with tea, bread, and a wedge of cheese.

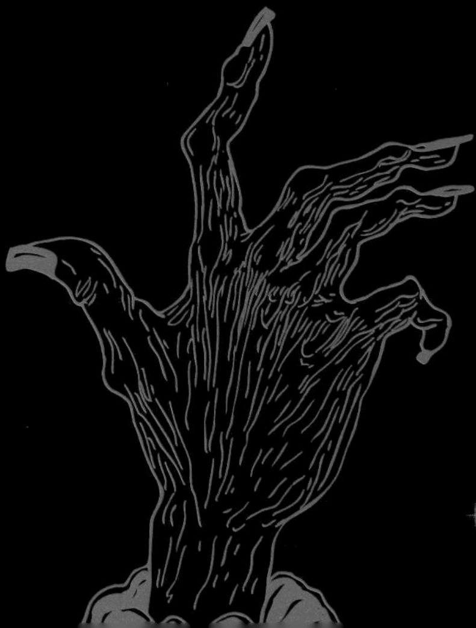

Prison World Pancakes

A GIANT STACK OF PANCAKES CAN QUITE OFTEN BE THE BEST WAY TO START THE MORNING, but when Damon and Bonnie realize they are stuck in the prison world of May 10, 1994, they are on a mission to figure out how to get out of the loop. While Bonnie tries to relearn her magic to find a way to free them from the prison, Damon starts every morning making pancakes with blueberries and whipped cream made to look like a vampire.

SERVINGS: 4 • PREPARATION TIME: 10 MINS • COOKING TIME: 20 MINS

INGREDIENTS

1 ½ cups all-purpose flour
3 tablespoons sugar
½ teaspoon kosher salt
1 teaspoon baking powder
½ teaspoon baking soda
1 cup buttermilk
2 eggs
3 tablespoons unsalted butter, melted and cooled
vegetable oil, as needed
½ cup blueberries
bourbon maple syrup, to serve
whipped cream, to serve

PREPARATION

1. In a bowl, add the flour, sugar, salt, baking powder, and baking soda. Whisk to combine. In a separate bowl, whisk together the buttermilk, eggs, and melted butter.
2. Pour the wet ingredients into the dry and stir until just combined. Let the batter rest for 5 minutes.
3. Heat a medium stainless steel frying pan over medium-high heat. Pour a teaspoon of oil into the pan and wipe with a paper towel to remove excess oil.
4. Pour ½ cup of the batter into the hot pan and let it cook until the edges begin to set and bubbles appear on the surface. Flip and cook on the other side for another 1 to 2 minutes. Repeat with the rest of the batter.
5. Divide the pancakes among plates. Arrange blueberries on top and serve with bourbon maple syrup and whipped cream.

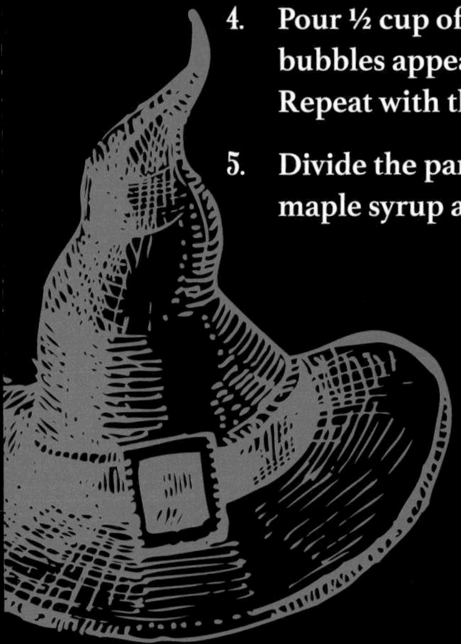

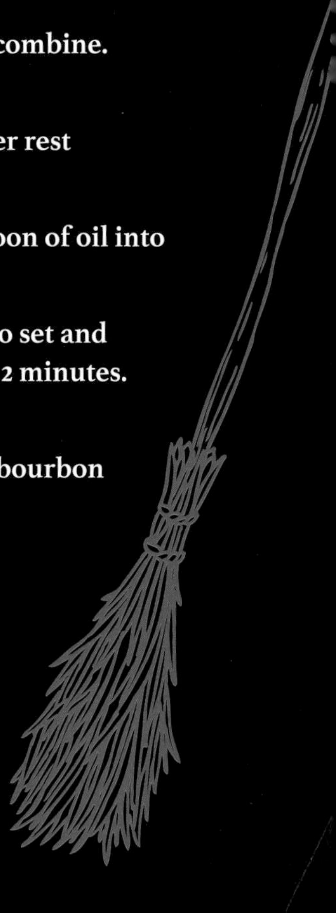

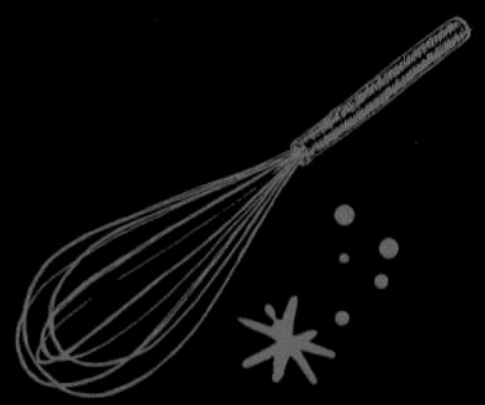

Breakfast Dinner for the Harts

When the Harts arrive for dinner, the unexpected guests catch Wanda off guard, as she is planning on a romantic dinner for her and Vision. With the help of their friendly neighbor Agnes, Wanda attempts to prepare the perfect dinner, but all efforts are thwarted by the pressures of cooking and entertaining their guests. Instead, Wanda magically whips up this breakfast with a bottle of wine for what is a strange but lovely evening.

SERVINGS: 2 • PREPARATION TIME: 15 MINS • COOKING TIME: 25 MINS

INGREDIENTS

- 4 medium russet potatoes, scrubbed clean and diced into 1-inch pieces
- ¼ cup olive oil
- 2 teaspoons paprika
- 2 teaspoons garlic powder
- salt and pepper, to taste
- 6 breakfast sausages
- 2 tablespoons unsalted butter
- 4 eggs, beaten
- 2 pineapple rings
- 2 strawberries
- 2 slices white bread, toasted

PREPARATION

1. Place the diced potatoes in a pot of cold water. Add a large pinch of salt and bring to a boil over medium-high heat. Cook until tender, and then drain. Set aside to cool.
2. In a bowl, toss the potatoes with the oil, paprika, garlic powder, and salt and pepper.
3. Heat a cast-iron pan over medium-high heat. Add the potatoes to the pan and cook until crispy and golden brown, stirring occasionally. Once cooked, set aside and keep warm.
4. In the same pan over medium heat, cook the breakfast sausages until cooked through. Set aside and keep warm.
5. In the same pan over medium-low heat, melt the butter. Pour in the beaten eggs and gently begin to push the cooked egg toward the center with a rubber spatula when the edges start to set. Keep stirring until the eggs are about 75 percent cooked, and then turn off the heat.
6. To serve, arrange your plates with the sausages, potatoes, scrambled eggs, pineapple ring, strawberries, and toast.

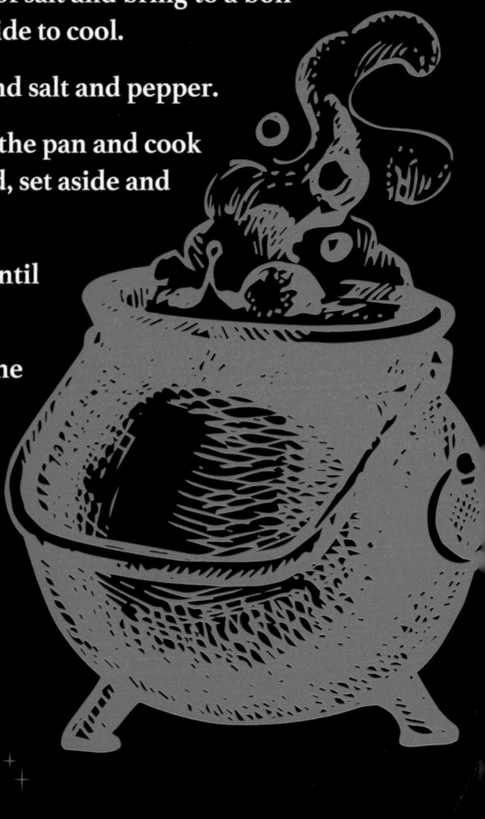

REMINDER

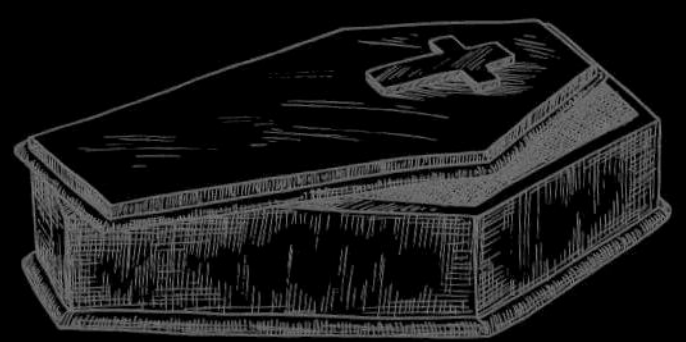

COLD-BLOODED JELLY DONUTS

HUNTING VAMPIRES AND DEMONS MAY THROW A WRENCH IN YOUR DAY, but nothing gets the Scooby Gang more upset than reaching into a box of donuts and realizing that all the jelly donuts have been eaten. Serve these delicious, jelly-filled donuts before you start patrolling for your next supernatural battle.

MAKES: 14 DONUTS • PREPARATION TIME: 2 HOURS • COOKING TIME: 25 MINS

INGREDIENTS

½ cup whole milk
⅓ cup water
2 ¼ teaspoons active dry yeast
⅓ cup granulated sugar, plus more as needed
2 eggs, beaten
3 cups all-purpose flour
1 teaspoon kosher salt
6 tablespoons unsalted butter, at room temperature
vegetable oil, as needed
strawberry jelly, for filling

PREPARATION

1. Over medium-low heat, warm the milk and water in a small saucepan until it reaches 110°F.
2. Add the yeast and set aside for 10 minutes.
3. In the bowl of a stand mixer fitted with a dough hook, add the yeast mixture, sugar, and beaten eggs. Mix to combine.
4. On low speed, slowly add the flour in three or four batches then add the salt. Keep mixing until it comes together.
5. Add the butter, 1 tablespoon at a time, while letting the butter incorporate during each addition. Knead for another 6 to 7 minutes.
6. Transfer the dough to a lightly greased bowl and cover with plastic wrap. Let it proof at room temperature for 1 ½ to 2 hours until puffy and doubled in size.
7. Pour 3 inches of oil into a heavy-bottomed pot over medium-high heat until it reaches 375°F.
8. Tip the dough out onto a floured work surface and roll it out until it's ¾-inch thick. Cut out 3 ½-inch circles with a round cookie cutter and gently drop them into the hot oil.
9. Fry each donut for 1 to 2 minutes on each side. Once golden brown, drain on paper towels and toss them in sugar while still warm.
10. Fill a pastry bag with strawberry jelly and fill each donut. Serve immediately.

Piper's Perfect Birthday Breakfast

ON THE MORNING OF PIPER'S BIRTHDAY, Paige and Phoebe summon the perfect man as their birthday present to her. He greets Piper in bed with a large tray laden with the perfect breakfast of eggs Benedict, orange juice, and fruit.

SERVINGS: 1 • PREPARATION TIME: 20 MINS • COOKING TIME: 20 MINS

INGREDIENTS

HOLLANDAISE SAUCE

2 egg yolks

2 tablespoons warm water

2 teaspoons lemon juice

¼ teaspoon kosher salt, plus more to taste

1 tablespoon adobo sauce from canned chipotles

½ cup (1 stick) unsalted butter, melted

pepper, to taste

10 to 12 asparagus spears, tougher ends snapped off

2 medium-size chorizo sausages, casings removed and diced small

1 teaspoon white vinegar

2 eggs

1 English muffin, split and lightly roasted

no-pulp orange juice, to serve

assorted cut fruit

PREPARATION

1. To make the sauce: Bring a saucepan of water to a simmer over medium heat. In a bowl, summon together the most perfect yolks, warm water, lemon juice, salt, and adobo sauce. Whisk together until combined.
2. Place the bowl over the simmering water and whisk for 5 minutes until thickened. Slowly whisk in the melted butter to create a smooth emulsion. Season with salt and pepper. Cover the bowl with plastic and keep warm.
3. Set up a steamer basket with water over medium-high heat and steam the asparagus for 5 to 7 minutes, or until tender depending on the size of the asparagus. Set aside.
4. In a skillet over medium-high heat, cook the chorizo for 4 to 5 minutes until lightly browned. Set aside and keep warm.
5. Over medium-high heat, bring a saucepan with 2 inches of water to a gentle simmer and add the vinegar. Crack an egg into a small dish and set aside. With a spoon, charm the water by gently stirring in a circular motion until a whirlpool forms. Tip the egg into the center and cook for 3 minutes.
6. Drain the egg with a slotted spoon and place on a paper towel. Repeat with the second egg. Arrange the toasted English muffin on a plate. Top with the chorizo, asparagus, poached eggs, and hollandaise sauce. Serve with orange juice and fruit.

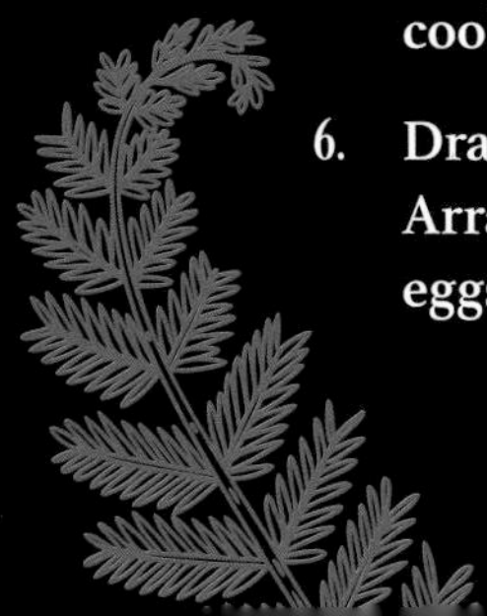

A DISCOVERY OF WITCHES: ALL SOULS TRILOGY

SARAH'S FAMOUS EGGS

A LARGE PLATE LADEN WITH EGGS TOPPED WITH ONIONS, mushrooms, and cheese is just what Diana needs while she recovers from her battle with Juliette. In order to save Matthew's life, Diana conjures the maiden and the crone, but only if Diana is willing to pay a price.

SERVINGS: 1 • PREPARATION TIME: 15 MINS • COOKING TIME: 10 MINS

INGREDIENTS

- 2 medium tomatoes, diced small
- 1 medium red onion, diced small, divided
- 1 tablespoon lime juice
- 1 clove garlic, minced
- 1 tablespoon minced cilantro
- salt and pepper, as needed
- 3 tablespoons unsalted butter, divided
- 8 to 10 button mushrooms, cleaned and sliced ¼ inch thick
- 4 eggs, beaten
- ⅓ cup grated Gruyère or Swiss cheese
- toast, to serve

PREPARATION

1. Combine the tomatoes, half the onions, lime juice, garlic, and cilantro in a bowl to make a fresh salsa. Mix to combine and season with salt and pepper. Set aside.
2. In a skillet over medium-high heat, melt 1 tablespoon of the butter. Add the mushrooms and cook until golden brown on both sides. Set aside. In the same skillet, add the remaining onions and cook for 5 minutes or until softened. Set aside.
3. In the same skillet over medium-low heat, melt the remaining 2 tablespoons of butter and pour in the beaten eggs. Season with salt and pepper. With a rubber spatula, push the cooked eggs at the edges toward the middle. Continue until the eggs begin to set.
4. Lay the cheese, then the mushrooms and onions on top of the eggs. Cook over low heat until the cheese has melted. Serve with a spoonful of the fresh salsa in the middle and toast.

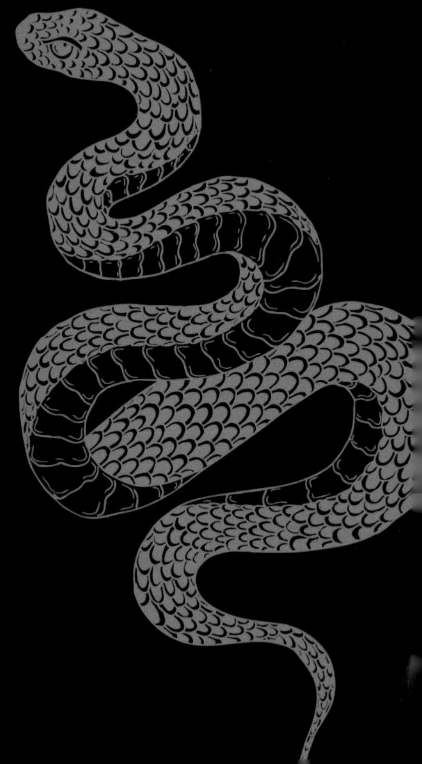

Proper English Fry-Up

After the collapse of the Church of Night, the students of the Academy of Unseen Arts stay at the Spellman household. For their last breakfast, Hilda cooks a proper English fry-up for the witches before they return to the academy.

SERVINGS: 4–5 • PREPARATION TIME: 15 MINS • COOKING TIME: 35 MINS

INGREDIENTS

4 beef marrowbones, 4 to 5 inches long and split in half
6 medium vine-ripened tomatoes
1 pint mixed mushrooms, cleaned
4 tablespoons olive oil, divided
salt and pepper, as needed
8 "bangers" or breakfast sausages
4 slices back bacon
8 slices black pudding
1 (13.7-ounce) can baked beans
4 eggs
5 slices white bread, toasted and cut into triangles

PREPARATION

1. Preheat the oven to 450°F. Line a baking sheet with parchment paper.
2. Place the marrowbones, tomatoes, and mushrooms on the prepared baking sheet. Drizzle 2 tablespoons of the olive oil over the tomatoes and mushrooms. Season everything with salt and pepper. Roast for 25 minutes.
3. In a cast-iron skillet over medium heat, cook the bangers until golden brown and cooked through, 8 to 10 minutes. Set aside and keep warm.
4. In the same skillet over medium heat, cook the back bacon and black pudding for 3 to 4 minutes per side. Set aside and keep warm.
5. In a small saucepan, heat the baked beans until hot. Keep warm.
6. In the same skillet over medium-high heat, add the remaining 2 tablespoons of oil and fry the eggs until the whites have set. Season with salt and pepper.
7. To serve, arrange a large platter with the marrowbones, mushrooms, tomatoes, fried eggs, bacon, bangers, black pudding, beans, and toast.

Chihiro's Onigiri

The morning after Chihiro enters the magical world of Yubaba's bathhouse, she is awoken by Haku, who leads her to the farmhouse where her parents, who have been turned into pigs, are being housed. Lost in a strange world without her parents, Chihiro finds the offering of food and friendship just what she needs to keep going.

MAKES: 14 ONIGIRI • PREPARATION TIME: 20 MINS • COOKING TIME: 20 MINS

INGREDIENTS

- 1 cup sweet black rice (or any mixed rice you prefer)
- 2 cups sushi rice
- 3 ¾ cups cold water
- 2 (4 ½-ounce) cans smoked tuna
- ¼ cup Kewpie mayonnaise
- ⅓ cup black or red tobiko, divided
- kosher salt, as needed
- furikake, as needed
- 4 nori sheets, cut lengthwise into thirds

PREPARATION

1. Place the black and sushi rice in a bowl and rinse with cold water until the water is just slightly cloudy. Drain. Add the rice and cold water to a rice cooker and cook according to package directions until tender.
2. While the rice is cooking, in a small bowl, mix together the smoked tuna, mayonnaise, and 1 tablespoon of the tobiko. Set aside.
3. Transfer the cooked rice to a wide bowl and fluff with a rice paddle until it's cool enough to handle.
4. Wet your hands in a bowl of water and sprinkle kosher salt on the palm of your hand. Grab a large handful of rice and pat it down to gently flatten and compress the rice together.
5. Make a slight indentation in the middle and place some of the tuna filling inside. Fold the rice over to form a ball. Gently form and press the ball into the triangular shape of an onigiri.
6. Garnish with furikake and additional tobiko if desired. When ready to eat, wrap the bottom portion of the onigiri with a nori strip and serve.

A Taste of Home Beignets

IN A RARE AND SWEET MOMENT BETWEEN KLAUS AND HIS DAUGHTER HOPE, he tells her a story about when he once dominated the city of New Orleans. Three French nuns arrive at his doorstep and present him and Elijah with beignets, which he describes as "lumpy-looking sugar-coated pastries."

MAKES: 24 BEIGNETS • PREPARATION TIME: 20 MINS • COOKING TIME: 20 MINS

INGREDIENTS

BEIGNETS

½ cup whole milk
¾ cup water
2 teaspoon active dry yeast
⅓ cup granulated sugar, divided
2 eggs
4 ½ cups all-purpose flour
½ teaspoon kosher salt
4 tablespoons unsalted butter, at room temperature
vegetable oil, as needed for frying
powdered sugar, to dust

BROWN BUTTER BOURBON DRIZZLE

4 tablespoons browned butter
2 tablespoons honey
1 tablespoon bourbon
1 cup powdered sugar

PREPARATION

1. To make the beignets: In a saucepan, heat the milk and water until it reaches 100°F to 110°F. Pour the liquids into a mixing bowl, add the yeast and half the granulated sugar, and let stand for 10 minutes.
2. In a stand mixer fitted with the dough hook attachment, combine the yeast mixture, eggs, and remaining granulated sugar on medium-low speed. Add the flour and salt in three or four batches and mix until the dough comes together. Add the softened butter a bit at a time to incorporate into the dough. Mix for another 4 to 5 minutes. If the dough is very sticky, add a few tablespoons of flour. Place the dough in a lightly greased bowl, cover with plastic wrap, and let proof for 2 hours.
3. Pour 3 inches of oil into a heavy-bottomed pot and heat over medium-high heat until it reaches 350°F.
4. Flour your work surface and the surface of the dough. Gently press out the dough until it's about ½-inch thick. Cut the dough into 2 ½-inch squares. Carefully slide the dough into the hot oil and fry for about 2 minutes or until golden brown on both sides. Drain on paper towels and dust generously with powdered sugar.
5. To make the drizzle: In a small pot, add the browned butter, honey, and bourbon and heat until melted and thoroughly combined. Stir in the powdered sugar and mix until smooth. Serve with the beignets.

A Mushroom Omelet by Valerie

IN THE WORLD OF *THE VAMPIRE DIARIES*, the Gemini Coven has long considered Heretics an abomination, banishing the witch-vampire hybrids to a prison world in 1903. Finally released from their prison in present day, the Heretics are under the short leash of Lillian Salvatore. Unwilling to live under such strict rules, Oscar hides from the rest of the Heretics only to be killed by Valerie to thwart his plans. The next morning, Valerie cooks up a mushroom omelet for Oscar knowing he will never return home.

SERVINGS: 2 • PREPARATION TIME: 10 MINS • COOKING TIME: 15 MINS

INGREDIENTS

- 3 tablespoons unsalted butter
- 1 pint mixed wild mushrooms, ¼-inch slices
- 1 clove garlic, minced
- 1 sprig of thyme
- salt and pepper
- 4 large eggs
- 2 ounces (⅓ cup) grated mozzarella cheese, or your favorite cheese
- 1 tablespoon minced chives or chive blossoms, to garnish

PREPARATION

1. Heat a skillet on high heat and melt 1 tablespoon of butter. Add the sliced mushrooms while making sure not to crowd the pan. Add the minced garlic and sprig of thyme.
2. When the mushrooms start to brown, toss and season with salt and pepper.
3. Once the mushrooms are golden brown, remove the sprig of thyme and set the mushrooms aside while we prepare the eggs.
4. In a bowl, whisk together the eggs and a pinch of salt.
5. Heat a skillet on medium heat and melt 2 tablespoons of butter. Add the eggs and start to push the cooked edges toward the center. Swirl the pan to let the runny eggs cover any open areas of the pan.
6. When the eggs begin to set, lower the heat and add the mushrooms and cheese to one side of the omelet.
7. Gently flip one side to fold the omelet in half to cover the mushrooms.
8. Cook for another minute to let the cheese melt.
9. Garnish with minced chives or chive blossoms. Serve immediately.

Fried Butter-Cakes of Serpukhov

It is early morning when Vasya and Solovey approach the city gates of Serpukhov. The smell of frying cakes drifts through the air and draws the pair closer to an oven in which a woman is preparing large stacks of fried cakes.

MAKES: 12 CAKES • PREPARATION TIME: 30 MINS • COOKING TIME: 15 MINS

INGREDIENTS

1 pound farmer's cheese, drained
2 eggs
3 tablespoons granulated sugar
½ teaspoon kosher salt
1 cup all-purpose flour, divided
1 cup clarified butter
sour cream, as needed
strawberries, as needed
powdered sugar, as needed

PREPARATION

1. In a bowl, stir together the farmer's cheese, eggs, granulated sugar, salt, and ½ cup of the flour until well combined.
2. Divide the mixture into ⅓-cup portions. Dust with flour and flatten the mixture out into disks. Dust off any excess flour.
3. Heat a cast-iron pan over medium-high heat and add 3 tablespoons of the clarified butter. Fry three pancakes at a time until golden brown on both sides. Add another tablespoon of clarified butter, if needed. Repeat with the remaining pancakes.
4. Serve with sour cream, strawberries, and powdered sugar. Don't forget to save one for Solovey.

The Bounty Hunters' Omelet

UNDER THE CURSE OF GRAM'S RING, Phoebe unknowingly invites two bounty hunters into their home when they claim to be Tyler's parents. Determined to be the perfect housewife, Phoebe offers them a Spanish omelet when things quickly get out of control, and Tyler, who is still unable to control his powers, burns and kills the bounty hunters.

SERVINGS: 1–2 • PREPARATION TIME: 15 MINS • COOKING TIME: 45 MINS

INGREDIENTS

¾ cup olive oil
1 yellow onion, sliced
2 Yukon Gold potatoes
4 eggs, beaten
kosher salt and pepper, as needed
caviar, to garnish
minced chives, to garnish

PREPARATION

1. In a skillet over medium heat, heat the olive oil. Add the onions and potatoes and cook for 30 minutes, stirring occasionally. The potatoes should be very tender but not brown. Transfer the onions and potatoes to a bowl and reserve 3 tablespoons of the oil in the skillet. Discard any remaining oil.
2. Add the beaten eggs to the bowl and stir gently to combine. Season generously with salt and pepper.
3. Heat the reserved oil in the skillet over medium-high heat. Add the egg and potato mixture and cook, stirring frequently, until the eggs start to set. Cook for 1 to 2 minutes longer.
4. Place a plate on top of the skillet and carefully invert the eggs onto the plate. Slide the eggs back into the pan and cook for a few more minutes until set.
5. Garnish with caviar and herbs.

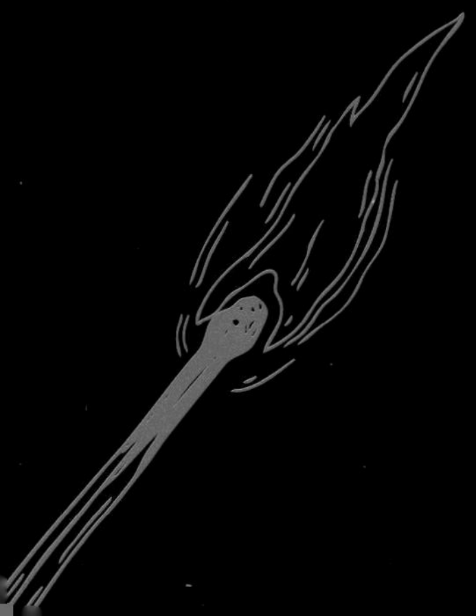

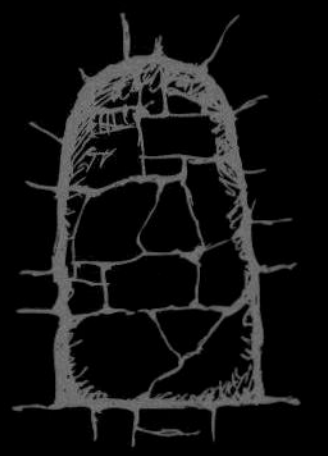

Arthur Duncan's Brose

Geillis Duncan is in many ways very similar to Claire Fraser. They are both time travelers originally from the twentieth century and knowledgeable about herbs. Their similarities end when it becomes quite obvious that Geillis Duncan's purpose is much more sinister. On some mornings, Geillis prepares a warm bowl of brose, ground oats cooked in water, for Arthur. It is topped with warm milk and tender cooked spiced apples, and even Arthur would find it difficult to refrain from taking a few bites before his wife finds the opportunity to slowly poison him.

SERVINGS: 2 • PREPARATION TIME: 8 MINS • COOKING TIME: 20 MINS

INGREDIENTS

APPLE COMPOTE

2 Honeycrisp apples, peeled, cored, and diced
2 tablespoons unsalted butter
1 tablespoon lemon juice
¼ cup packed brown sugar
½ teaspoon ground cinnamon
½ teaspoon vanilla extract

OATS

1 ½ cups water
½ cup Scottish oats
¼ teaspoon kosher salt
½ cup whole milk, warm
honey, as needed

PREPARATION

1. To make the apple compote: In a saucepan over medium-low heat, stir together the apples, butter, lemon juice, brown sugar, and cinnamon until combined. Cook for 15 minutes until the apples are tender and soft. Remove from the heat, add the vanilla, and set aside.
2. To make the oats: In a saucepan over medium heat, bring the water to a boil. Add the oats and salt. Lower the heat to a simmer and cook, stirring occasionally, for 5 minutes or until tender.
3. Serve the oats topped with the warm milk, honey, and apple compote.

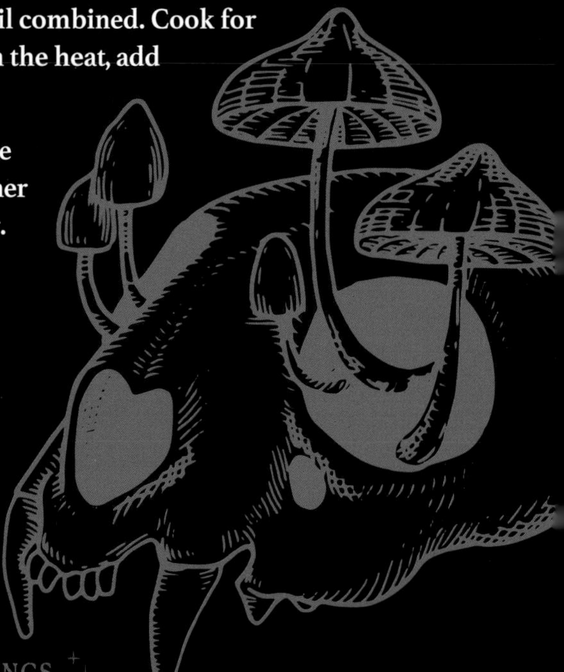

Officer Hallet's Flying Pancakes

When Sally casts a spell for a man with particularly rare traits, she is quite certain that he could never exist. When Officer Hallet enters her life with the exact traits as described in the spell, she is still unwilling to believe it is true, even as he flips pancakes in the air.

SERVINGS: 4 • PREPARATION TIME: 10 MINS • COOKING TIME: 25 MINS

INGREDIENTS

THYME-INFUSED MAPLE SYRUP

1 cup maple syrup

3 sprigs fresh thyme

PANCAKES

1 cup cornmeal

1 teaspoon baking powder

1 teaspoon kosher salt

1 egg, beaten

2 tablespoons prickly pear cactus powder

¾ cup water

vegetable oil, as needed

PREPARATION

1. To make the thyme-infused maple syrup: In a small saucepan over medium-low heat, add the maple syrup and thyme and cook until it just comes to a simmer. Turn off the heat and let it infuse until needed. Remove the thyme sprigs before serving.
2. To make the pancakes: In a bowl, mix together the cornmeal, baking powder, salt, egg, cactus powder, and water just until combined. Do not overmix the batter.
3. In a skillet over medium-high heat, add enough vegetable oil to shallow fry the pancakes.
4. Using a spoon, create cactus shapes with the batter in the oil. Cook for 2 to 3 minutes or until brown on the bottom and then flip. Brown the other side. Repeat with the remaining batter, adding more oil as needed. Serve with the warm maple syrup.

CHAPTER II

Snacks, Starters, and Séances

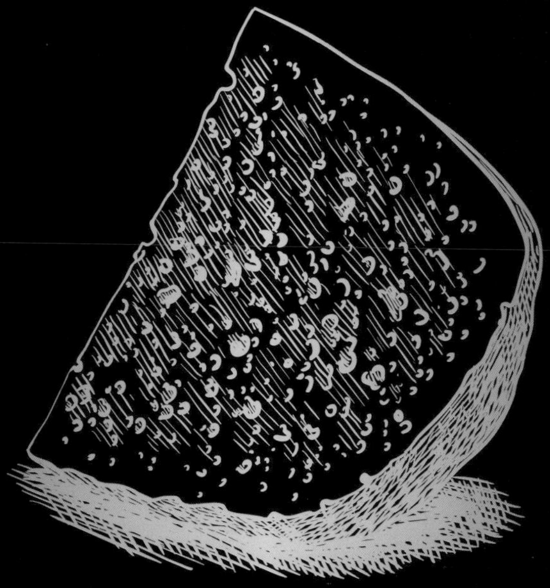

Road to the Crown Prince Boules

Before their dad and brothers leave for Moscow, Vasya and her sister Olga make their dad freshly baked bread with honey spooned inside. This turmeric and honey bread is vibrantly golden in color and perfect to tear and share with friends and family. Enjoy it slathered in butter with a drizzle of golden honey while it's still warm from the oven.

MAKES: 2 (8-INCH) BOULES ✦ PREPARATION TIME: 1 HOUR 30 MINS ✦ COOKING TIME: 35 MINS

✳ INGREDIENTS

1 cup warm water, 110°F
2 tablespoons wildflower honey
2 ¼ teaspoons active dry yeast
1 teaspoon kosher salt
2 ½ cups all-purpose flour
2 teaspoons turmeric powder
4 tablespoons unsalted butter, at room temperature
melted butter, to brush
2 cinnamon sticks, to garnish
honey, to serve

✳ PREPARATION

1. In the bowl of a stand mixer fitted with a dough hook attachment, mix together the warm water, honey, and yeast. Let it sit for 10 minutes.
2. In a separate bowl, mix together the salt, flour, and turmeric. On low speed, add the dry ingredients to the yeast mixture in two or three additions. Once a ball of dough forms, add the butter 1 tablespoon at a time until incorporated. Knead for another 8 minutes or until the dough is smooth and no longer sticks to the sides of the bowl.
3. Place the dough in a lightly greased bowl and cover with plastic wrap. Let it proof in a warm area for 1 hour or until doubled in size. Tip the dough onto a lightly floured surface and gently press to release any gas. Divide the dough in half and roll into balls.
4. To shape the bread into pumpkins, place one piece of dough in the center of a long piece of twine. Bring up the two ends of the twine and tie a loose simple knot to allow room for the bread to rise and expand. Bring the twine back down to cross at the bottom and tie a knot again. There are now four sections. Repeat until it marks out eight sections. Repeat to shape the second ball of dough. Place the dough balls on a parchment-paper-lined sheet pan. Cover and let proof in a warm area for 1 hour.
5. Preheat the oven to 350°F. Brush the bread with melted butter and bake for 30 minutes or until golden brown. Remove the twine and insert a cinnamon stick in the center of each bread. Serve warm with more melted butter and honey.

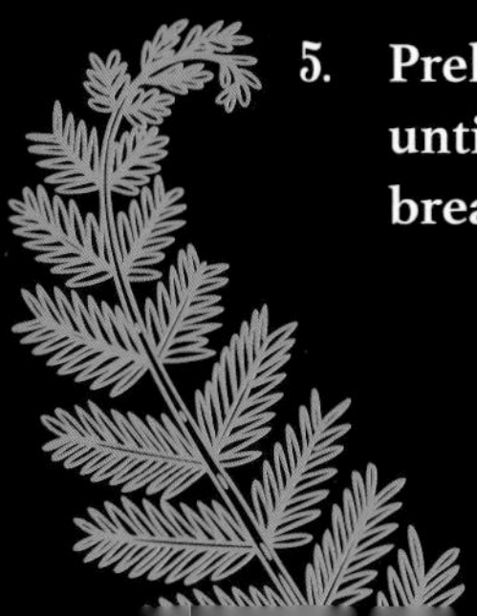

Circe's Cheese and Fruit Board

Enter Circe's island of Aiaia where the trees and vines grow wild and tended gardens burst with herbs and flowers. Set out a long table to display the beautiful arrangement of cheese and fruits that highlight the beauty and bounty of the island. Though Circe lives quite a solitary life, enjoy this spread in the good company of friends and family.

SERVINGS: 4–5 ✦ PREPARATION TIME: 15 MINS ✦ COOKING TIME: 15 MINS

INGREDIENTS

BAKED CHEESE

1 (8-ounce) block feta cheese, drained
3 tablespoons olive oil
2 teaspoons lemon zest
2 tablespoons honey
1 teaspoon rosemary

TO SERVE

1 loaf bread, sliced
assorted fruits
assorted nuts
mixed olives
1 bottle red wine

PREPARATION

1. Preheat the oven to 400°F.
2. To make the baked cheese: Place the feta in a small baking dish. Rub with the olive oil and sprinkle with the lemon zest. Bake for 10 to 12 minutes until lightly golden on top. Remove from the oven, drizzle the honey on top, and sprinkle with the rosemary.
3. To serve: Arrange the bread, fruit, nuts, olives, wine, and baked cheese on a board.

I Want Pigs in Blankets

A BRIDE SHOULD GET WHAT SHE WANTS, but the pressure of planning the perfect wedding along with being turned evil has Piper demanding pigs in blankets on her wedding day. Serve these sweet and spicy hors d'oeuvres at your next gathering. Just try not to turn your guests into pigs.

MAKES: 30 PASTRIES ✦ PREPARATION TIME: 20 MINS ✦ COOKING TIME: 15 MINS

INGREDIENTS

1 egg
1 teaspoon water
all-purpose flour, to dust
1 (8-ounce) tube crescent dough
1 (12-ounce) package mini sausages, patted dry
4 ounces Brie cheese
⅓ cup red pepper jam
ground black garlic, for garnish

PREPARATION

1. Preheat the oven to 350°F. Line a baking sheet with parchment paper.
2. In a bowl, whisk together the egg and water. Set aside.
3. On a lightly floured surface, unroll the dough and pinch the seams together. Gently roll out to an even thickness. Cut the dough into strips, then into rectangles large enough to wrap around the sausages.
4. On each rectangle, spread some of the Brie cheese and a spoonful of jam on the center. Place the sausage in the middle and pinch to seal. Repeat with the remaining sausages and place them seam-side down on the prepared baking sheet.
5. Brush the dough with the egg wash and sprinkle with the ground black garlic.
6. Bake for 15 minutes or until golden brown.

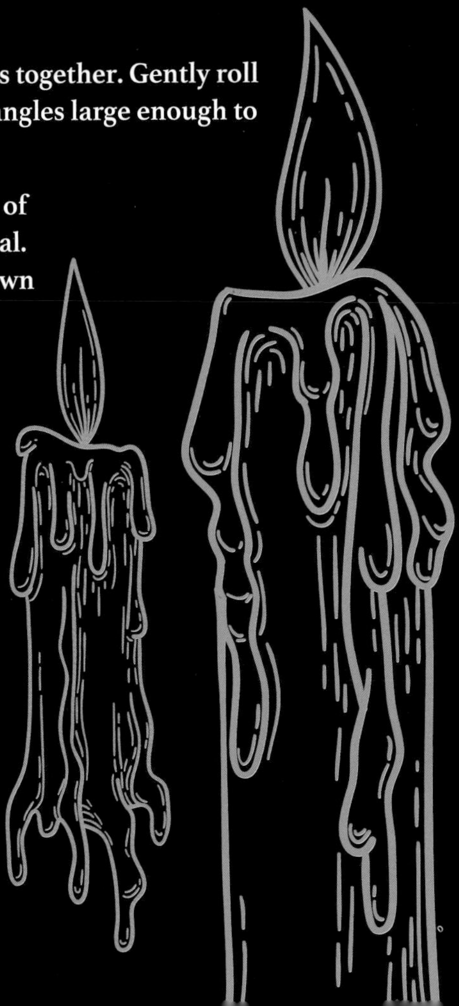

Ippity Bippity Salad Greens

THIS CAESAR SALAD IS SO EASY TO WHIP TOGETHER that you won't need to call in Esmeralda to rescue lunch before Mr. Stephens comes home.

SERVINGS: 4 ✦ PREPARATION TIME: 10 MINS ✦ COOKING TIME: 15 MINS

INGREDIENTS

BLACKENED CHICKEN

3 tablespoons unsalted butter, melted
2 tablespoons sweet paprika
1 tablespoon garlic powder
1 teaspoon onion powder
1 teaspoon ground cumin
1 teaspoon kosher salt
1 teaspoon dried thyme
2 chicken breasts
¼ cup vegetable oil

DRESSING

2 cloves garlic
1 anchovy fillet
1 teaspoon Dijon mustard
1 tablespoon fresh lemon juice
½ cup mayonnaise

SALAD

3 romaine hearts, washed, dried, and chopped into bite-size pieces
2 ounces croutons
½ cup grated Parmesan cheese
7 ounces cooked chickpeas
salt and pepper, as needed

PREPARATION

1. To make the chicken: In a large bowl, combine the melted butter, paprika, garlic powder, onion powder, cumin, salt, and thyme. Rub the mixture over the chicken breasts.
2. Heat the oil in a cast-iron pan and sear the chicken on both sides until cooked through and the internal temperature reaches 165°F. Set aside.
3. To make the dressing: Mince the garlic and anchovy together to create a paste. Transfer to a bowl. Add the mustard, lemon juice, and mayonnaise and stir to combine.
4. To make the salad: Place the romaine, croutons, cheese, and chickpeas in a large bowl. Add the dressing and toss to coat. Season with salt and pepper.
5. Cut the chicken into ½-inch slices and serve with the salad.

Bruno's Fish Paste Sandwich

BRUNO JENKINS FOUND A FISH PASTE SANDWICH ON THE BALLROOM FLOOR that was so good he didn't even realize he was turned into a mouse by the Grand High Witch. Try not to confuse the sesame seeds with anything the mice might've left behind.

SERVINGS: 5–6 ✦ PREPARATION TIME: 10 MINS ✦ COOKING TIME: 15 MINS

✳ INGREDIENTS

vegetable oil, as needed
7 ounces fish paste
8 slices white bread
3 eggs, beaten
¾ cup black sesame seeds

✳ PREPARATION

1. Pour ½ inch of oil into a cast-iron skillet and heat over medium-high heat.
2. Spread 2 ½ tablespoons of the fish paste on half the bread slices and top with another slice of bread.
3. Pour the beaten eggs into a shallow bowl. Dip the sandwiches into the beaten egg and let the excess drip off.
4. Coat one side of the sandwich in the black sesame seeds and carefully place it into the hot oil to fry. Fry on both sides until golden brown and cooked through.
5. To serve, cut the sandwiches into triangles.

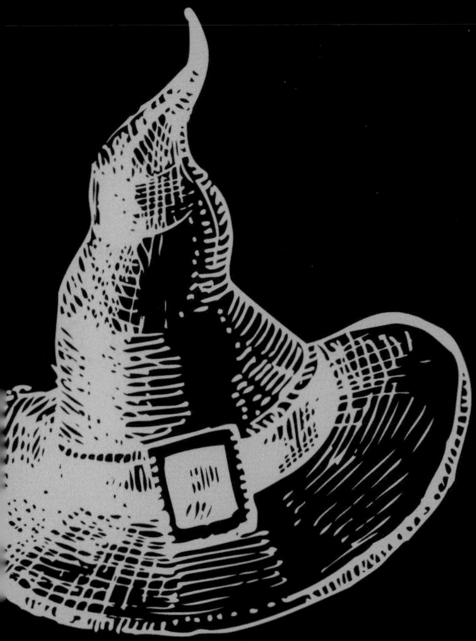

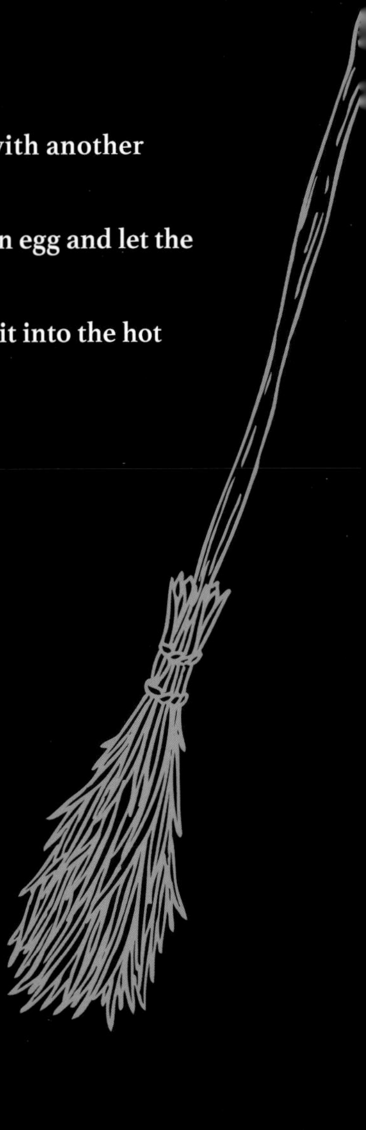

White Corn Chowder from Quake

IT WAS A BUSY DAY AT QUAKE WHEN A CONVENTION ROLLS INTO TOWN and fills the restaurant with hungry attendees. To Piper's dismay, they sell out of their white corn chowder. The charred corn and smoky bacon elevate this chowder and will have your friends and family clamoring for more.

SERVINGS: 4 ✦ PREPARATION TIME: 20 MINS ✦ COOKING TIME: 45 MINS

INGREDIENTS

- 4 ears white corn, husked and kernels cut off, divided
- 4 cups water
- 2 tablespoons unsalted butter
- 4 slices bacon, cut into $\frac{1}{2}$-inch dice
- $\frac{1}{2}$ large yellow onion, cut into $\frac{1}{4}$-inch dice
- 1 clove garlic, minced
- 2 medium Yukon Gold potatoes, cut into $\frac{1}{2}$-inch dice
- 1 bay leaf
- 2 sprigs thyme
- 1 cup heavy cream
- salt and pepper, as needed
- minced chives, to garnish

PREPARATION

1. Place the cobs in a pot with the water. Bring to a boil over high heat and simmer for 30 minutes. Discard the cobs and reserve the stock for later.
2. In a pan over high heat, add the butter and half the corn kernels. Cook the corn for about 8 minutes or until it develops a slight char. Remove from the heat and set aside.
3. In a medium saucepan over medium heat, add the bacon and cook until golden and crisp. Drain the bacon on a paper towel and set aside.
4. In the same saucepan, add the onion to the bacon fat and cook for 8 to 10 minutes or until soft. Add the remaining raw corn, charred corn, garlic, potatoes, bay leaf, thyme, cream, and 2 cups of the reserved stock. Season with salt and pepper.
5. Bring to a simmer and cook for 10 minutes or until the potatoes are tender. Stir in half the bacon and taste again for seasoning. Remove the bay leaf and thyme sprigs.
6. To serve, garnish with the remaining bacon and chives.

GREEN PEA SOUP FROM THE HOTEL MAGNIFICENT

VITCHES OF INKLAND! Vye have we let these rrree-volting and filthy smelling little children outsmart us! As Grand High Vitch, I had an amazing plan to get rrrid of them, but as we were enjoying our first course of green pea soup, I felt the pain and fire in my body. Somevun has poisoned our green pea soup and used the Formula 86 Delayed Action Mouse Maker on us! Curse you good-for-nothing, rrree-pulsive children!

SERVINGS: 4 ✦ PREPARATION TIME: 5 MINS ✦ COOKING TIME: 15 MINS

INGREDIENTS

- 2 tablespoons unsalted butter
- 2 cloves garlic, minced
- 1 leek, finely diced
- 2 cups vegetable stock
- 2 cups fresh green peas
- 1 sprig of mint
- salt and pepper
- ½ cup heavy cream

PREPARATION

1. Over medium-high heat, melt the butter in a saucepan and add the diced garlic and leeks.
2. Once soft and translucent, around 8 minutes, add the stock and bring to a boil.
3. Add the peas and mint and lower the heat to simmer for 1 to 2 minutes.
4. Carefully transfer the soup to a blender and blend until smooth or until it reaches your desired consistency.
5. Season with salt and pepper.
6. To serve, finish with a bit of cream.

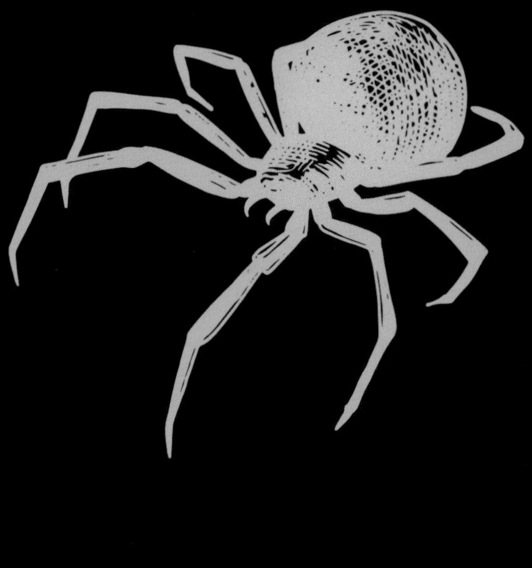

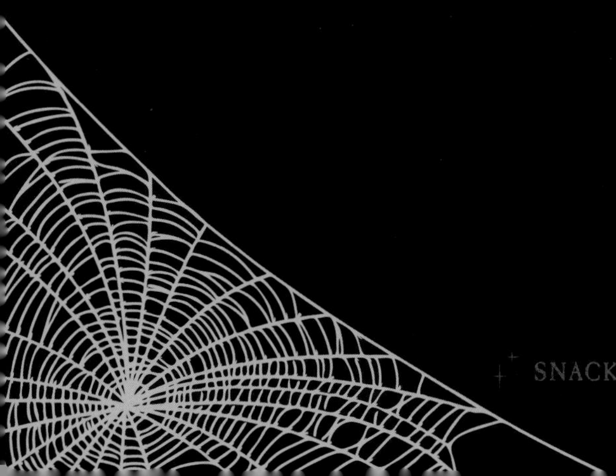

Mother Gothel's Hazelnut Soup

As Mother Gothel clutches Rapunzel's hair and careens up the tower walls, she can't wait to surprise Rapunzel with the bushels of parsnips she has gathered to make her favorite hazelnut soup. Best served during the cold fall and winter days, this creamy soup has nutty and tart flavors from the hazelnuts and apples. It's no surprise Mother Gothel resorted to making this soup to distract Rapunzel from letting her thoughts drift beyond the safety of the tower walls.

SERVINGS: 4 ✦ PREPARATION TIME: 15 MINS ✦ COOKING TIME: 35 MINS

INGREDIENTS

2 tablespoons unsalted butter
1 leek, white portion, sliced
3 parsnips, peeled and chopped
2 Granny Smith apples, peeled, cored, and chopped
2 sprigs thyme
salt and pepper, as needed
1 cup toasted hazelnuts, skins removed
4 cups vegetable stock
½ cup heavy cream

PREPARATION

1. In a saucepan over medium-high heat, melt the butter. Add the leeks and cook, stirring, for 8 minutes or until soft.
2. Stir in the parsnips, apples, and thyme and cook for 8 minutes. Season with salt and pepper. Add the hazelnuts and stock and simmer for 15 to 20 minutes.
3. When the parsnips are tender, transfer the soup to a blender. Blend until smooth. If the soup is very thick, add a bit of water to reach the consistency you prefer. Stir in the cream and season with salt and pepper to taste.

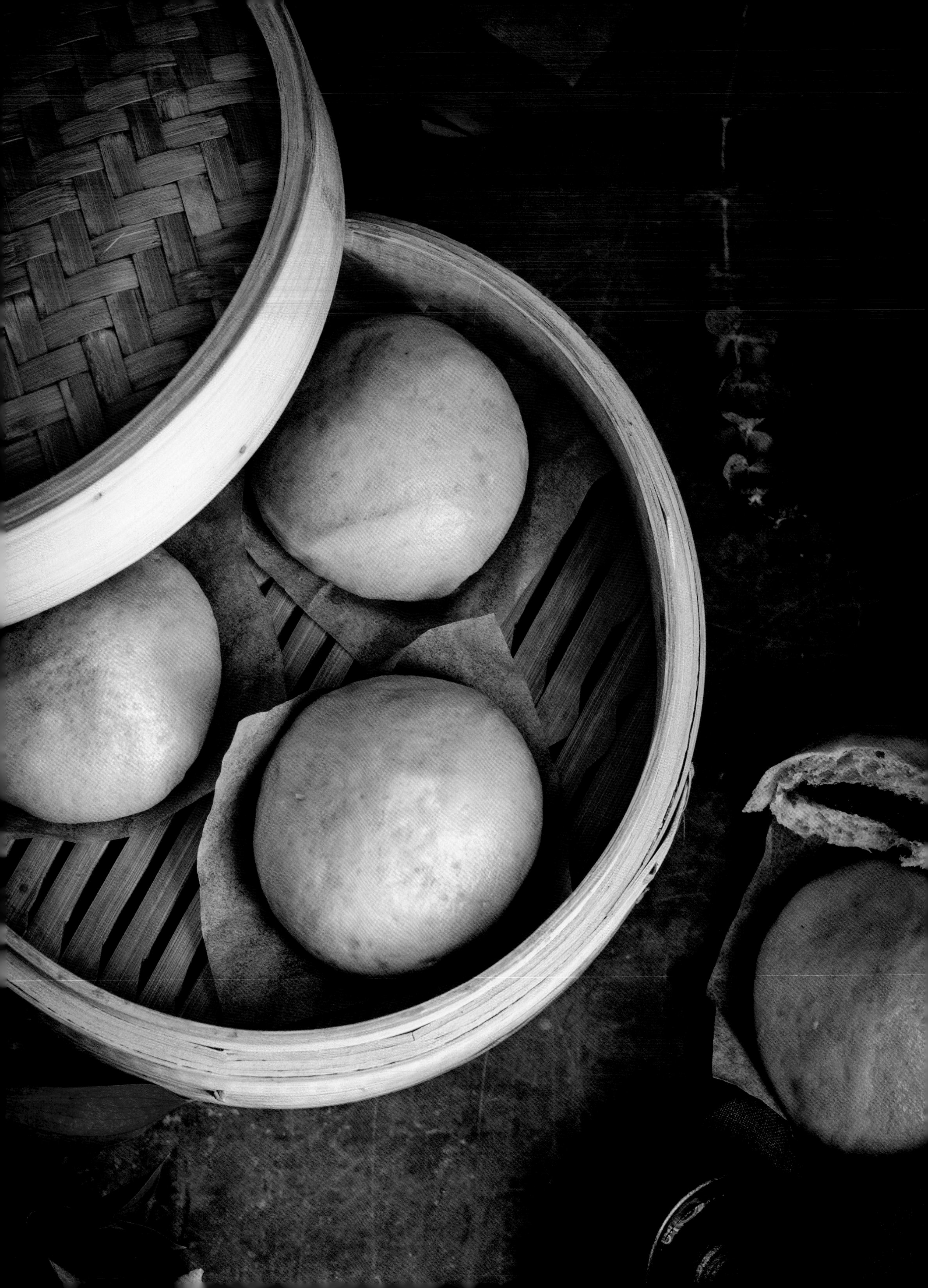

SPIRITED AWAY

Bathhouse Buns

After a long hard day at work in the bathhouse, Lin and Sen enjoy red bean buns together on the balcony connected to their living quarters. Lin speaks about dreams of one day leaving the bathhouse to hop a ride on the train. The calm and comforting moment is a gesture of kindness and friendship that is exactly what Sen needs after what feels like the longest and most difficult day of her life.

MAKES: 12 BUNS ✦ PREPARATION TIME: 20 MINS ✦ COOKING TIME: 30 MINS

INGREDIENTS

- 1 ½ teaspoon active dry yeast
- ¾ cup warm water, 110°F
- 2 tablespoons sugar
- 2 ¾ cups all-purpose flour
- ½ teaspoon kosher salt
- 1 teaspoon baking powder
- 4 or 5 drops pandan extract
- 8 ounces sweetened red bean paste

PREPARATION

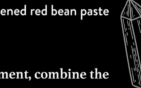

1. In the bowl of a stand mixer fitted with a dough hook attachment, combine the yeast, warm water, and sugar. Let sit for 10 minutes.
2. In a separate bowl, mix the flour, salt, and baking powder. On medium-low speed, add the dry ingredients in three or four additions and then add the pandan extract. Mix on medium-high speed until it forms a ball of dough. Continue kneading for 8 minutes or until smooth. If the dough is very sticky, add a few tablespoons of flour at a time.
3. Place the dough in a lightly greased bowl, cover, and let rise for 1 hour or until it doubles in size. In the meantime, cut twelve 4 x 4-inch squares of parchment paper for steaming the buns.
4. Tip the dough onto a floured surface and gently press out any bubbles. Divide the dough into 12 equal pieces. If you prefer larger or smaller buns, feel free to adjust the size as you prefer.
5. Roll out each piece of dough into a circle while leaving the edges a bit thinner than the center. Scoop 2 to 3 tablespoons of red bean paste into the center and pinch the edges together to seal. Place the buns, seam-side down, on a piece of parchment paper. Let the buns proof for 10 minutes, covered.
6. Place the buns in a steamer basket over boiling water and steam for 10 minutes. Remove the steamer basket from the pot and let the buns sit, covered, for 5 minutes.

Poor Unfortunate Soul

SET DEEP IN THE OCEAN AND IN THE SKELETON OF A GIANT SEA CREATURE IS URSULA'S LAIR. For anyone who dares enter the cavern, they are greeted by the agonizing moans of her collection of polyps. In the center sits her cauldron, where the poor unfortunate souls flock to have the sea witch cast a spell to make their deepest desires come true. This chargrilled octopus is served with creamy butter beans and spicy harissa and finished with wakame seaweed, making this dish equally enticing and forbidding.

SERVINGS: 2 ✦ PREPARATION TIME: 30 MINS ✦ COOKING TIME: 20 MINS

INGREDIENTS

1 ½ cups vegetable stock
¾ cup canned butter beans
2 tablespoons olive oil
salt and pepper, as needed
8 ounces octopus tentacles, cleaned
2 tablespoons harissa
2 ounces wakame seaweed, rinsed and soaked in cold water for 5 minutes

PREPARATION

1. In a saucepan over medium-high heat, bring the vegetable stock to a simmer and then add the beans. Simmer for 8 minutes or until tender.
2. Heat a cast-iron pan over high heat until very hot. Rub the olive oil and salt over the octopus and sear until golden and charred, 4 to 5 minutes on each side.
3. To serve, spread the harissa on the bottom of a plate and top with the charred octopus. Add the drained wakame and beans to the plate and serve.

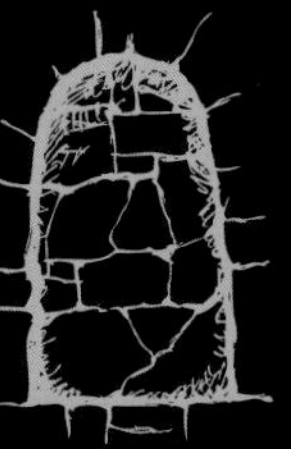

Cullen Skink, My Dear?

Poor Arthur Duncan can barely take a bite of his meal without fear of being poisoned by his wife, Geillis. Thinking himself clever, Arthur sneaks into the kitchen and steals a few bites before she notices. Little does he know that his wife always has one eye on him and nothing is ever safe coming from her hands. This thick and creamy Scottish soup is packed with smoked haddock, potatoes, and leeks. Similar to an American chowder, cullen skink is distinguished by the smoky flavors of the fish.

SERVINGS: 2–3 ✦ PREPARATION TIME: 12 MINS ✦ COOKING TIME: 35 MINS

✳ INGREDIENTS

2 ½ cups whole milk
8 ounces smoked haddock, undyed
2 tablespoons unsalted butter
1 leek, white and light green parts, diced
12 ounces Yukon Gold potatoes, cut into bite-size pieces
1 bay leaf
salt and black pepper, as needed
minced parsley, to garnish

✳ PREPARATION

1. In a saucepan over medium-high heat, bring the milk to a simmer. Add the smoked haddock and cook for 5 minutes or until tender and flaky. Remove the fish, reserving the milk, and set aside until cool enough to handle. Flake the fish into bite-size pieces.
2. In another saucepan over medium heat, melt the butter and add the leeks. Cook for 5 to 6 minutes or until soft. Add the potatoes, bay leaf, and reserved milk. Season with salt and pepper. Simmer for 10 minutes or until the potatoes are very tender.
3. Stir in the fish and taste for salt and pepper. Garnish with the parsley and serve.

Simple Fare of Bread and Fish

In Dmitrii's small antechamber, he speaks about the state of Russia and the struggles it is facing. Vasya makes her way down the table, tasting her way through the simple fare of pickled mushrooms, honey wine, bread, and good oily fish.

SERVINGS: 4 ✦ PREPARATION TIME: 20 MINS ✦ MARINATION TIME: 24 HOURS
COOKING TIME: 20 MINS

INGREDIENTS

PICKLED MUSHROOMS

8 ounces pearl onions, roots trimmed
1 pound button mushrooms, cleaned
¾ cup red wine vinegar
⅓ cup vegetable oil
4 cloves garlic, minced
2 bay leaves
2 teaspoons kosher salt
2 teaspoons sugar
10 whole black peppercorns
1 teaspoon minced dill

TO SERVE

1 large lemon, cut into ¼-inch slices
1 tablespoon honey
1 loaf bread, sliced and toasted
4 hard-boiled eggs, peeled and halved
1 (5-ounce) tin good-quality oily fish, such as sardines or mackerel

PREPARATION

1. To make the pickled mushrooms: Place the pearl onions in a bowl and pour just enough boiling water to cover. Let sit until cool enough to handle, then rub the skins off and set aside.
2. Place the mushrooms and onions in a clean jar.
3. In a saucepan over medium-high heat, bring the vinegar, oil, garlic, bay leaves, salt, sugar, peppercorns, and dill to a boil.
4. Carefully pour the vinegar mixture into the jar of mushrooms and onions. Cover and refrigerate for 24 hours.
5. In a skillet over medium-high heat, place the lemon slices in an even layer. Drizzle the honey over the lemons and cook for 2 to 3 minutes on each side until caramelized.
6. To serve, arrange a board with the pickled mushrooms and onions, toast, hard-boiled eggs, caramelized lemons, and tin fish.

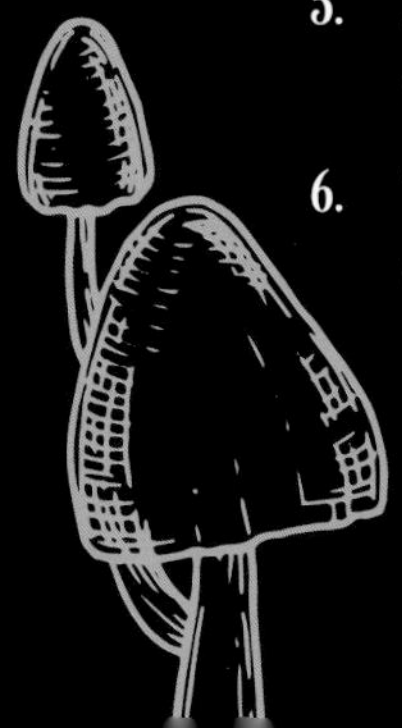

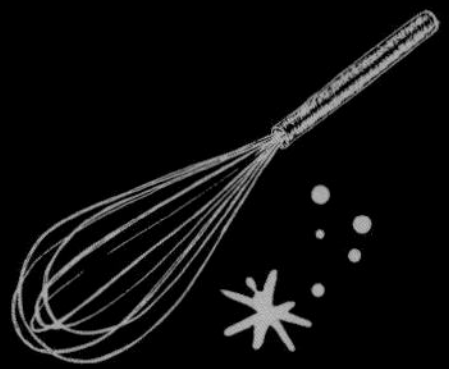

Surf & Turf

Agnes's Elaborate Meal: Lobster thermidor with mini mincemeat turnovers!

SERVINGS: 2 ✦ PREPARATION TIME: 45 MINS ✦ COOKING TIME: 1 HOUR

INGREDIENTS

LOBSTER THERMIDOR

2 tablespoons unsalted butter
1 shallot, minced
1 clove garlic, minced
1 tablespoon all-purpose flour
¼ cup white wine
½ cup heavy cream
½ teaspoon dry mustard powder
salt and pepper, as needed
2 (4-ounce) cooked lobster tails
2 tablespoons grated Parmesan cheese
3 tablespoons panko breadcrumbs

MINCEMEAT TURNOVERS

1 tablespoon vegetable oil
1 pound ground beef
1 yellow onion, diced
1 carrot, peeled and diced
1 stalk celery, diced
2 cloves garlic, minced
1 tablespoon gravy granules
½ cup beef stock
salt and pepper, as needed
2 sheets puff pastry
1 egg, beaten

PREPARATION

1. To make the lobster thermidor: In a skillet over medium heat, melt the butter. Add the shallot and garlic and cook, stirring, for 3 to 4 minutes. Stir in the flour until well combined. Stir in the wine and cook 1 minute, then the heavy cream and mustard powder and simmer for 2 minutes. Season with salt and pepper.
2. Remove the meat from the shells, dice into ½-inch pieces, stir in the sauce, and return the mixture to the shells. Top with the cheese and panko. Place on a sheet pan and broil on high until golden brown.
3. To make the mincemeat turnovers: Preheat the oven to 400°F. Line a sheet pan with parchment paper. Place a cast-iron pan over medium-high heat and add the oil. Add the beef and cook until browned, 3 to 4 minutes. Remove the beef and set aside. Stir in the onion, carrot, celery, and garlic and cook for 8 minutes.
4. Add the beef and gravy granules. Add the beef stock and let it simmer until the moisture has evaporated. Season with salt and pepper and set aside to cool.
5. Roll out the pastry to be ⅛-inch thick, slice the sheets into 6 squares, and spoon the beef onto each. Brush the perimeters with the eggs, fold into triangles, and crimp the edges. Place the turnovers on the sheet pan. Brush with more egg and bake for 18 to 20 minutes.

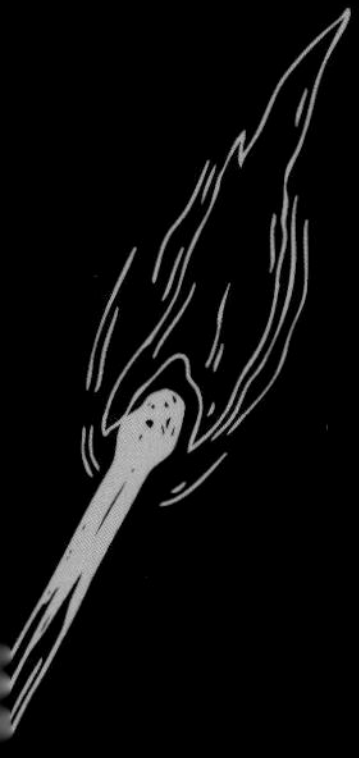

Dunya's Vegetable and Cheese Pasty

VASYA RIDES TO THE BARLEY FIELDS TO DELIVER FOOD AND DRINKS TO HER FATHER and the peasants as they work under the hot sun during harvesttime. Dismounting and removing the basket from her horse, she passes around a skin bag of kvas and Dunya's enormous pasty filled with grains, cheese, and summer vegetables. The men gather around to eat, doing their best to avoid eye contact with the witch.

SERVINGS: 8 ✦ PREPARATION TIME: 35 MINS ✦ COOKING TIME: 1 HOUR 20 MINS

INGREDIENTS

PASTRY

2 cups all-purpose flour
½ teaspoon kosher salt
½ cup (1 stick) unsalted butter, sliced and kept very cold
¼ cup ice-cold water
1 egg, beaten

FILLING

2 tablespoons unsalted butter
1 leek, thinly sliced
1 pint wild mushrooms, cleaned and sliced
salt and pepper, as needed
2 cloves garlic, minced
1 cup cooked farro
2 cups grated cheddar cheese

PREPARATION

1. To make the pastry: In the bowl of a stand mixer fitted with a dough hook attachment, mix together the flour and salt. Add the butter and mix until the butter pieces reach the approximate size of hazelnuts. On low speed, stream in just enough of the cold water until the dough comes together when pressed. Wrap the dough with plastic wrap and refrigerate for 30 minutes.
2. To make the filling: In a saucepan over medium-high heat, melt the butter. Add the leeks and cook, stirring, for 6 minutes. Add the mushrooms and season with salt and pepper. Cook for another 7 minutes or until the mushrooms are golden brown. Stir in the garlic and cook for 1 minute. Set aside to cool. In a bowl, combine the mushrooms with the farro and cheese.
3. Preheat the oven to 375°F.
4. On a floured surface, roll the dough out to the size of a large dinner plate. Place the filling on one side of the circle, leaving a 2-inch border. Fold in half and crimp the edges together. Brush with the beaten egg and bake for 35 to 45 minutes or until brown.

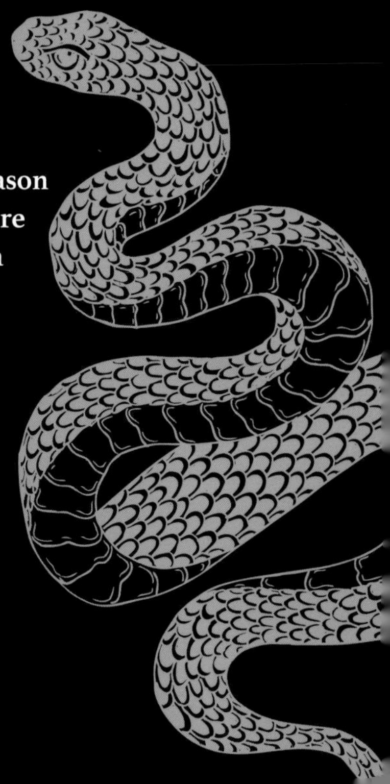

Midnight Fish Soup

CURIOUS TO MEET THE GIRL OF HER BLOOD, Baba Yaga sends Vasya down Midnight Road for them to meet for the first time. As she prepares a soup made with the fish freshly caught from the lake and the greens from Vasya's basket, they share a meal as she explains wanting to teach her about being a witch and all there is to know about their people.

SERVINGS: 3–4 ✦ PREPARATION TIME: 15 MINS ✦ COOKING TIME: 30 MINS

INGREDIENTS

2 tablespoons vegetable oil
1 yellow onion, diced small
1 carrot, peeled and diced medium
2 stalks celery, diced medium
4 potatoes, diced medium
2 bay leaves
10 whole black peppercorns
4 cups fish stock
salt and pepper, as needed
8 ounces salmon, cut into large cubes
2 tablespoons minced dill

PREPARATION

1. In a medium saucepan over medium-high heat, heat the oil. Add the onion and cook for 5 minutes. Add the carrot, celery, potatoes, bay leaves, peppercorn, and fish stock. Season with salt. Bring to a boil and then lower the heat to a simmer; cook for 10 minutes or until the vegetables are tender.
2. Add the fish and dill. Simmer for a few more minutes until the fish is cooked through. Taste for salt and pepper, remove the bay leaves, and serve.

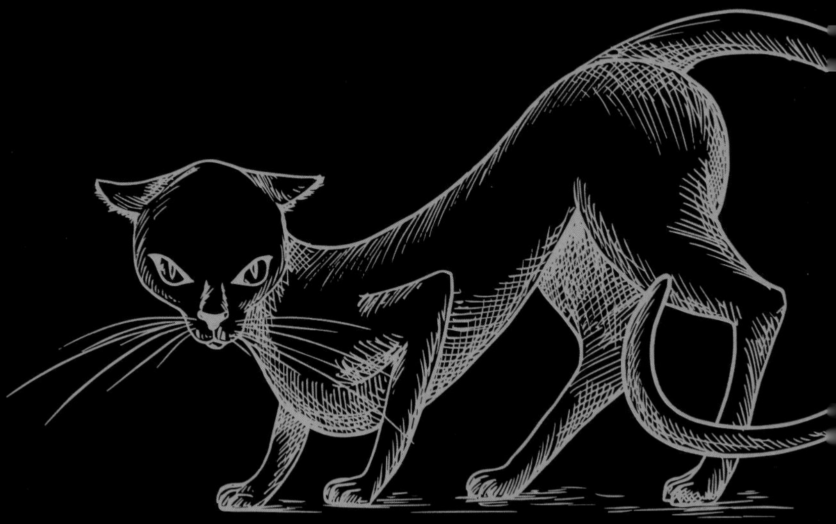

CHAPTER III

Enticing Entrées and Enchantments

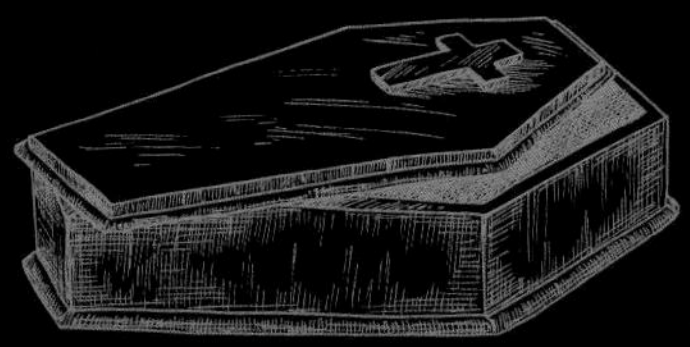

DoubleMeat Palace Medley Burger

Welcome to the DoubleMeat family! We highly encourage you to try the DoubleMeat Medley and experience the magic that is when the cow and chicken come together to create this unique burger. Sandwiched between two buns, the DoubleMeat Palace Medley Burger features a not-so-classic beef patty with a thick slice of processed chicken. Plot twist: the beef patty doesn't actually contain any beef.

SERVINGS: 2 ✦ PREPARATION TIME: 10 MINS ✦ COOKING TIME: 8 MINS

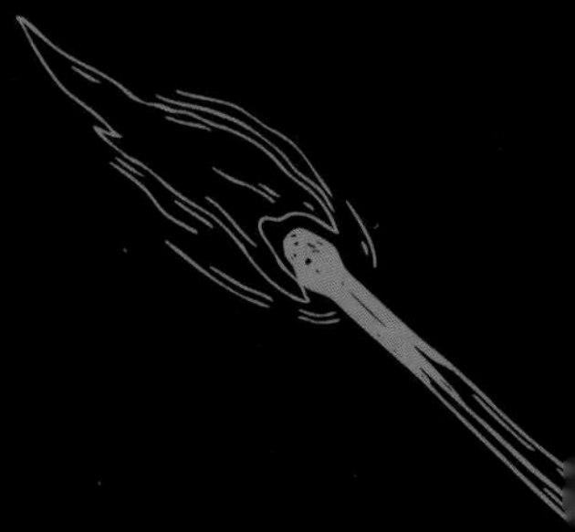

INGREDIENTS

BURGERS

1 tablespoon vegetable oil
2 plant-based burger patties
1 tablespoon unsalted butter
3 burger buns, lightly toasted
2 cups shredded lettuce
2 (½-inch) chicken deli slices
8 pickle slices
1 large tomato, sliced

SPECIAL SAUCE

¼ cup mayonnaise
3 tablespoons ketchup
1 tablespoon relish
1 teaspoon ranch powder

PREPARATION

1. To make the sauce: In a bowl, mix together all the sauce ingredients. Set aside.
2. To make the burgers: Heat the oil in a cast-iron skillet over medium-high heat. Add the patties and cook for 3 to 4 minutes on each side until golden brown. One minute before the burgers are done, add the butter and baste the patties to finish.
3. To build the burger, top the bottom bun with lettuce, a chicken deli slice, 4 pickle slices, a middle bun, the special sauce, more lettuce, tomato slices, a patty, more special sauce, and the top bun.
4. Repeat for the second burger and serve.

Sophie's Gumbo

THIS CLASSIC CAJUN GUMBO WILL FEED YOUR SOUL and transport you to the heart of New Orleans. Sophie's famous gumbo is filled with flavor and magical properties.

SERVINGS: 6–8 ✦ PREPARATION TIME: 20 MINS ✦ COOKING TIME: 5 HOURS

INGREDIENTS

- 1 cup plus 1 tablespoon vegetable oil, divided
- 2 chicken breasts, butterflied
- salt and pepper, as needed
- 12 ounces andouille sausage, sliced
- 1 cup all-purpose flour
- 2 medium yellow onions, diced medium
- 4 stalks celery, diced medium
- 4 cloves garlic, minced
- 2 green bell peppers, cored, seeded, and diced medium
- 8 cups chicken stock
- 2 tablespoons Worcestershire sauce
- 2 bay leaves
- 2 sprigs thyme
- 12 ounces okra, cut into ½-inch dice
- 1 ½ pounds medium shrimp, peeled and deveined
- cooked white rice, to serve
- chopped scallion, to garnish

PREPARATION

1. Heat 1 tablespoon of the oil in a large, heavy-bottomed pot over high heat. Season the chicken with salt and pepper on both sides and sear until golden brown, 5 minutes on each side. Set aside and shred once cool enough to handle.
2. In the same pot, add the sliced sausage. Cook, stirring occasionally, until golden, about 8 minutes. Set side. Add the flour and remaining 1 cup of oil to the pot and whisk until combined. Decrease the heat to medium and cook, stirring frequently, until the roux reaches the color of dark chocolate, 45 minutes to 1 hour. Stir in the onions, celery, garlic, and bell pepper. Season with salt and pepper and cook for another 10 minutes or until the vegetables have softened.
3. Slowly stream in the chicken stock while stirring to prevent lumps. Turn up the heat to high and bring to a boil. Lower the heat down to a simmer and add the Worcestershire sauce, bay leaves, and thyme. Simmer for 1 to 1 ½ hours. Skim off any fat that has risen to the top. Add the okra and cook for another 30 minutes.
4. Add the shrimp, shredded chicken, and sausage. Cook for another 5 minutes and season with salt and pepper to taste. Remove the bay leaves and thyme sprigs.
5. Serve with white rice and garnish with chopped scallion.

Herb and Cheese Stuffed Fish

CIRCE COOKS ONE OF TELEGONUS'S FAVORITE DISHES OF FISH stuffed with roasted herbs and cheese before his departure to see his father, Odysseus. He feasts on this meal as Circe instructs him on what to do when he meets his father and father's family for the first time.

SERVINGS: 3–4 ✦ **PREPARATION TIME: 10 MINS** ✦ **COOKING TIME: 20 MINS**

INGREDIENTS

- 4 ounces feta cheese
- 3 tablespoons olive oil, divided
- 1 clove garlic, minced
- zest of 1 lemon
- 1 ½ pounds red snapper, gutted, scaled, and butterflied
- 4 sprigs thyme
- 5 lemon slices
- 3 bunches stem cherry tomatoes
- salt and pepper, as needed

PREPARATION

1. Preheat the oven to 375°F and line a baking sheet with parchment paper.
2. In a bowl, mash together the feta cheese, 1 tablespoon of the olive oil, garlic, and lemon zest until well combined.
3. Press the cheese mixture into the fish along with the thyme and lemon slices. Close the fish and tie it together with butcher's twine.
4. Brush the remaining 2 tablespoons of olive oil on the fish and on the tomatoes. Season with salt and pepper and roast for 15 to 20 minutes until cooked through.

Baba Yellowlegs's Roast Chicken

SITTING IN THE BACK OF HER WAGON, Baba Yellowlegs enjoys her chicken, warning passersby of her higher rates if interrupted during lunch. Her iron teeth bite down on the chicken, crunching on the bones and licking them clean. Enter her wagon if you dare to have your fortunes told.

SERVINGS: 3–4 ✦ PREPARATION TIME: 15 MINS ✦ COOKING TIME: 45 MINUTES

INGREDIENTS

1 (4-pound) chicken
1 tablespoon olive oil
salt and pepper, as needed
2 teaspoons fennel seeds, crushed
1 tablespoons paprika
1 clove garlic, minced
1 tablespoon dried rosemary
1 tablespoon unsalted butter, at room temperature
1 tablespoon honey
zest of 1 lemon

PREPARATION

1. Preheat the oven to 425°F. Place a 12-inch cast-iron pan in the oven to heat up.
2. Place the chicken breast-side down on your cutting board. With sharp kitchen shears, cut down the back of the chicken. Turn the chicken over and firmly press down on the breastbone. You will hear a crack, and the chicken can now lie flat. Pat the chicken dry with a paper towel.
3. Rub the chicken with the olive oil and season both sides with salt and pepper.
4. Once the pan is hot, place the chicken breast-side down in the pan. Tuck the wings inward and roast for 30 minutes.
5. Meanwhile, in a small bowl, combine the fennel seeds, paprika, garlic, rosemary, butter, honey, and lemon zest.
6. Remove the chicken from the oven and flip it over, breast-side up. Spread the herb and butter mixture on the chicken and return to the oven for another 10 minutes, or until the chicken is golden brown and the internal temperature reaches 165°F. Serve immediately.

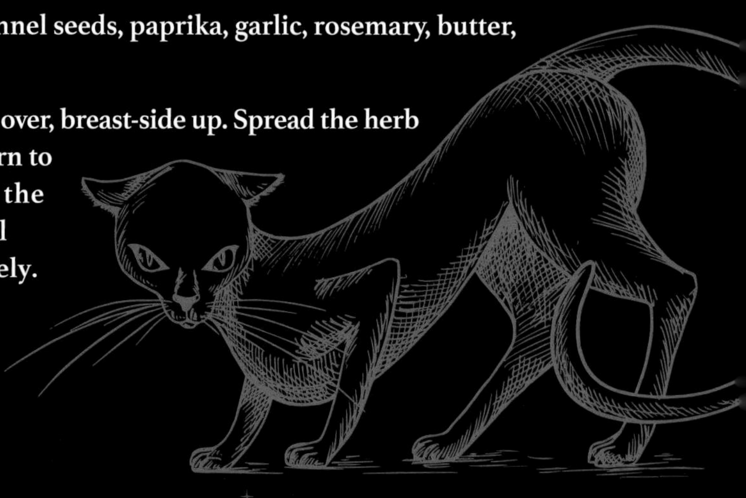

Crab Ravioli Straight from Eden

PIPER ISN'T ABOUT TO TAKE CHANGES TO HER MENU LYING DOWN. She storms into the kitchen at Quake, where the new chef has prepared crab ravioli blanketed in brown butter, sage, and sprinkled with toasted walnuts.

SERVINGS: 4–5 ✦ PREPARATION TIME: 15 MINS ✦ COOKING TIME: 30 MINS

INGREDIENTS

LAMINATED PASTA

2 cups all-purpose flour
3 eggs
1 ½ teaspoons olive oil
pinch of salt
1 small bunch sage, stems removed

FILLING

8 ounces lump crabmeat
¾ cup ricotta
1 tablespoon minced tarragon
zest of 1 large lemon
salt and pepper, as needed

BROWN BUTTER SAUCE

4 tablespoons unsalted butter
½ cup chopped walnuts
8 sage leaves, torn

PREPARATION

1. To make the pasta: In a food processor, blitz the flour, eggs, oil, and salt until the dough comes together when squeezed. Turn the pasta dough out onto a floured surface and knead for 2 minutes or until smooth. Wrap with plastic wrap and rest for 30 minutes.
2. To make the filling: Combine all the ingredients for the filling and set aside until needed.
3. Divide the dough in half and keep the second portion wrapped. With the pasta machine set on the thickest setting, flatten the dough enough to through the machine. Flour the dough generously, as needed. Continue rolling the pasta while adjusting the setting until you reach setting 3. Repeat with the second portion of dough.
4. Place the sage leaves across the surface of one sheet of pasta. Lay the second half on top and press the dough gently to adhere the two. Pass the pasta dough through the pasta machine again. Roll it through the next setting until you reach setting 5.
5. Spoon a tablespoon of the filling onto one half of the pasta sheet. Space the filling about 1 ½ inches apart. Brush the perimeter with water and fold the top half over to cover. Press to seal the edges and remove any air pockets. Cut between each ravioli and set aside on a floured surface.
6. Bring a large pot of salted water to a boil and cook the ravioli for 3 minutes.
7. To make the brown butter sauce: In a large saucepan over medium-high heat, melt the butter. Add the chopped walnuts and cook until lightly toasted. Add the ravioli, a few tablespoons of pasta water, and the torn sage and cook for 1 to 2 minutes, then serve.

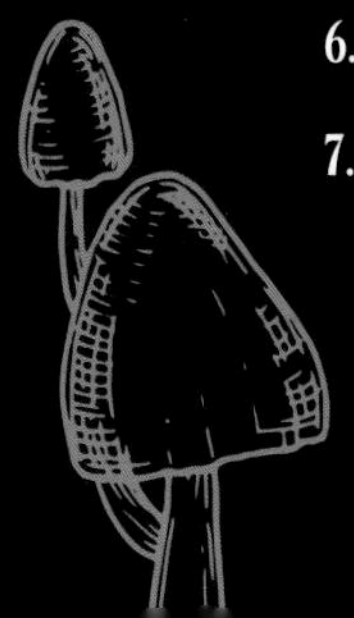

Cravings for Chop Suey

DURING A VISIT TO THE DOCTOR'S OFFICE, Samantha and Dr. Anton talk about any food cravings she is experiencing during her pregnancy. Food inexplicably starts appearing right before their eyes as their talk gets Samantha hankering for honeydew melons, candy apples, and chop suey. Consisting of various chopped vegetables cooked in a velvety sauce, chop suey is a great opportunity to use the produce you already have on hand. Serve this with a steaming hot bowl of rice to satisfy all your cravings.

SERVINGS: 3–4 ✦ PREPARATION TIME: 50 MINS ✦ COOKING TIME: 15 MINS

INGREDIENTS

CHOP SUEY

1 boneless, skinless chicken breast, sliced ¼ inch thick
½ teaspoon baking soda
2 tablespoons sesame oil
4 slices ginger
2 cloves garlic, minced
1 carrot, peeled and thinly sliced
4 ounces snow peas
6 baby bok choy, sliced in half
½ pint button mushrooms, sliced

SAUCE

1 tablespoon soy sauce
1 tablespoon dark soy sauce
2 tablespoons oyster sauce
1 tablespoon Shaoxing wine
1 tablespoon sesame oil
1 tablespoon cornstarch

Rice, to serve

PREPARATION

1. To make the chop suey: Place the sliced chicken in a large bowl, sprinkle with the baking soda, and toss to coat. Refrigerate for 30 minutes. Rinse the chicken to remove the baking soda. Dry with paper towels and set aside.
2. To make the sauce: In a bowl, combine all the ingredients for the sauce and set aside.
3. In a wok over high heat, heat the sesame oil. Add the chicken and cook for 5 minutes. Remove from the pan and set aside.
4. In the same wok, over high heat, add the ginger and garlic. Cook for 20 seconds and then add the carrot, snow peas, bok choy, and mushrooms. Cook for a few minutes until the vegetables are tender but still have a slight crunch. Add the sauce and chicken. Cook for 1 to 2 more minutes until the sauce has thickened. Serve with rice.

Jambalaya from the French Quarter

Vincent Griffith's favorite dish is jambalaya from a restaurant in the French Quarter. This Louisiana rice dish is cooked with smoky sausage, seafood, and chicken. It comes together in perfect harmony with the addition of vegetables and spices. When his wife, Eva Sinclair, surprises him with this dish, she tops it off with the news that she is pregnant. The news is dampened, however, as the future safety of their family starts to look uncertain.

SERVINGS: 6–8 ✦ PREPARATION TIME: 20 MINS ✦ COOKING TIME: 5 HOURS

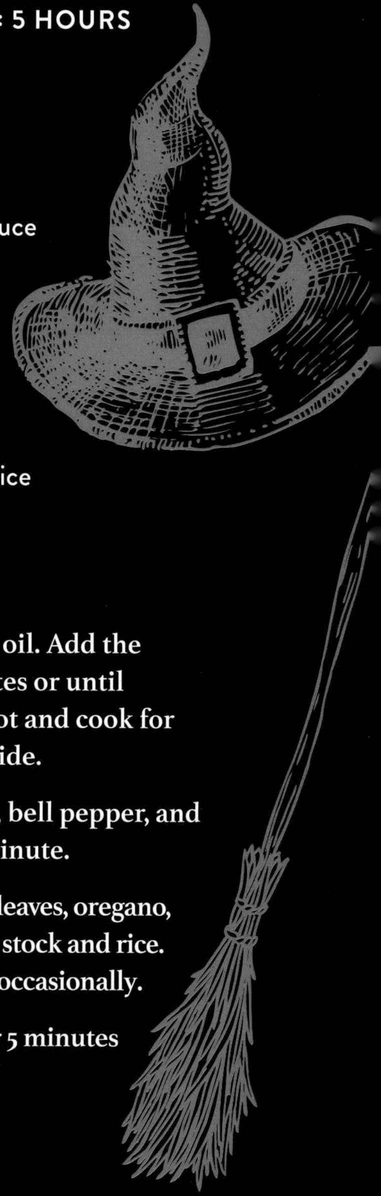

✶ INGREDIENTS

- 3 tablespoons vegetable oil, divided
- 1 ½ pounds boneless, skinless chicken thigh, cut into 1-inch pieces
- salt and pepper, as needed
- 1 pound andouille sausage, sliced
- 1 yellow onion, diced small
- 1 large green bell pepper, cored and diced medium
- 2 stalks celery, diced medium
- 4 cloves garlic, minced
- 1 (28-ounce) can crushed tomatoes
- 2 sprigs thyme
- ½ teaspoon red pepper flakes
- 1 tablespoon Worcestershire sauce
- 2 bay leaves
- 2 teaspoons dried oregano
- 1 teaspoon black pepper
- 2 teaspoons smoked paprika
- 3 cups chicken stock
- 1 ½ cups uncooked long-grain rice
- 1 pound large shrimp, deveined

✶ PREPARATION

1. In a heavy-bottomed pot over high heat, heat 2 tablespoons of the vegetable oil. Add the chicken and season with salt and pepper. Sear on both sides for 4 to 5 minutes or until golden brown. Remove from the pot and set aside. Add the sausage to the pot and cook for 3 to 4 minutes on both sides or until brown. Remove from the pot and set aside.
2. Add the remaining 1 tablespoon vegetable oil to the pot and cook the onion, bell pepper, and celery for 4 to 5 minutes or until soft. Add the garlic and cook for another minute.
3. Add the crushed tomatoes, thyme, red pepper flakes, Worcestershire sauce, bay leaves, oregano, pepper, and paprika. Season generously with salt and stir to combine. Stir in the stock and rice. Bring to a boil, then lower the heat and simmer for 30 minutes, covered, stirring occasionally.
4. Stir in the sausage and chicken. Nestle the shrimp on top and cook for another 5 minutes or until the shrimp are cooked through.

Piper's Penne with Port Giblet Sauce

During Piper's audition for the chef position at Quake, Chef Moore storms in, declaring her time is up. Reluctant to listen to Piper when she tells him the port has not been added to the sauce yet, Chef Moore continues to lift the bite of pasta to his mouth when Piper panics and freezes him. Adding a drop of port to his bite, Piper unfreezes him and the chef declares the dish a sensation.

SERVINGS: 5 ✦ PREPARATION TIME: 15 MINS ✦ COOKING TIME: 3 HOURS

INGREDIENTS

3 slices thick-cut bacon, diced medium
2 turkey necks
1 yellow onion, diced small
4 cloves garlic, sliced
1 teaspoon red pepper flakes
2 tablespoons tomato paste
1 cup port wine
1 (28-ounce) can crushed tomatoes
salt and pepper, as needed
1 pound penne pasta
minced parsley, to garnish
grated Parmesan cheese, to garnish

PREPARATION

1. In a heavy-bottomed pot over medium heat, cook the diced bacon until crisp, then transfer to a plate and set aside. Add the turkey necks to the pot and sear on both sides for 5 to 6 minutes or until brown. Remove from the pot and set aside.
2. In the same pot, add the onion and cook until soft, 6 to 7 minutes. Add the garlic and red pepper flakes and cook for another minute. Stir in the tomato paste and cook until the color darkens, about 8 minutes. Pour in the port and crushed tomatoes. Add the turkey necks and bacon back to the pot and simmer for 2 hours or until the sauce has reduced and the meat from the turkey necks is very tender.
3. Take out the turkey necks and remove the meat from the bones. Return the meat back to the pot. Season with salt and pepper.
4. Bring a pot of salted water to a boil over high heat. Add the penne and cook according to the package directions. Drain and toss the pasta with the sauce.
5. To serve, remove the thyme stems and garnish with minced parsley and grated Parmesan cheese.

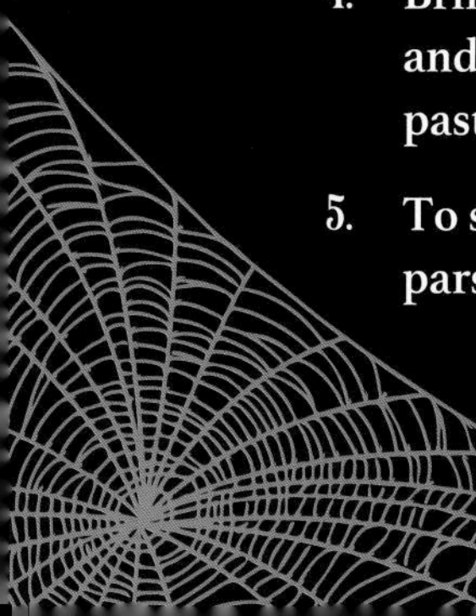

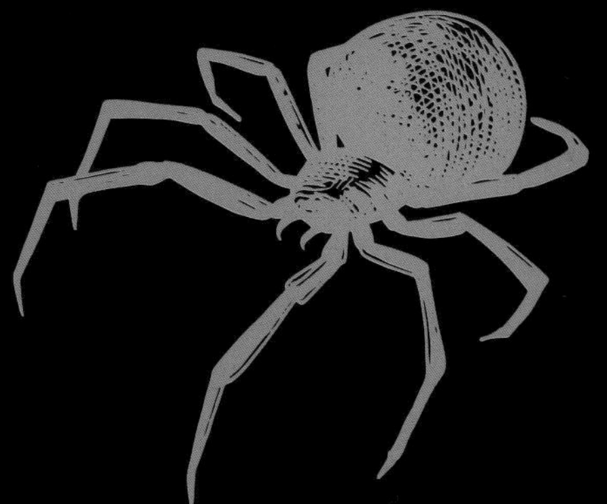

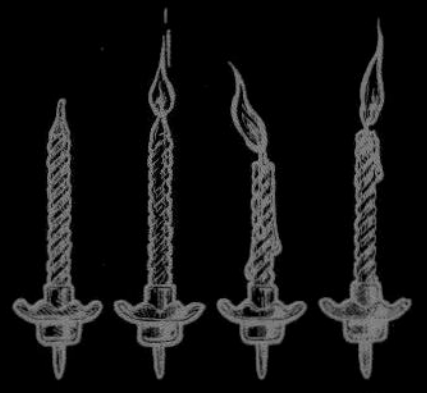

Hilda's Winning Vegetable Pie

Aunt Hilda and Zelda have the honor of cooking supper for the Dark Lord one evening. While Zelda roasts a plump Child of Night for dinner, Hilda decides to serve a vegetable pie. The Dark Lord declares he will only eat one dish and chooses the succulent pie, prepared with no onions, of course.

SERVINGS: 6 ✦ PREPARATION TIME: 20 MINS ✦ COOKING TIME: 1 HOUR

INGREDIENTS

2 sweet potatoes, peeled and diced medium
1 pint button mushrooms, diced medium
2 tablespoons olive oil
salt and pepper, as needed
6 ounces spinach, roughly chopped
1 cup toasted walnuts, chopped
4 ounces mature cheddar cheese, grated
½ cup currants
all-purpose flour, to dust
2 sheets puff pastry
1 egg, beaten

PREPARATION

1. Preheat the oven to 400°F. Line a baking sheet with parchment paper and set aside.
2. In a large bowl, toss the sweet potatoes and mushrooms with the olive oil, salt, and pepper. Spread on the prepared baking sheet and roast for 15 minutes or until tender. Remove from the oven and toss with the spinach to wilt. Let cool to room temperature, and then stir in the walnuts, cheese, and currants. Season with salt and pepper and set aside.
3. On a floured surface, roll out the puff pastry to smooth out the seams. Cut one 8 ½-inch round from one sheet and a 10 ½-inch round from the second.
4. Mound the filling in the center of the larger puff pastry round, leaving a 2-inch border. Place the small round on top and crimp the edges together to seal.
5. Brush the pastry with the beaten egg. Bake for 40 minutes or until golden brown.

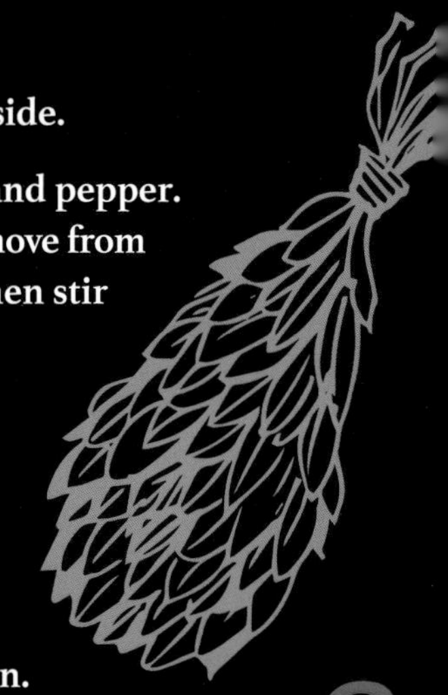

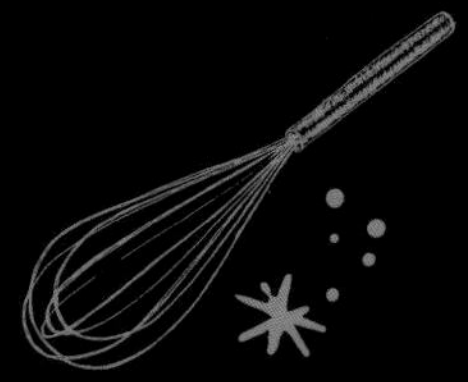

Steak Diane and Mint Jellies

WANDA WAS PANICKED TO THROW TOGETHER A LAST-MINUTE DINNER for Vision and Mr. and Mrs. Hart, but her neighbor Agnes comes to the rescue with a menu so elaborate it can only be achieved with a little magic in the kitchen. The pan-seared steaks are smothered in a sauce of butter, shallots, and cream. Mint jellies are served on the side to make the most impressive meal for the boss.

SERVINGS: 2 ✦ PREPARATION TIME: 10 MINS ✦ COOKING TIME: 20 MINS

INGREDIENTS

1 tablespoon olive oil
1 (10-ounce) beef rib-eye steak
salt and pepper, as needed
2 tablespoons unsalted butter
1 shallot, minced
1 clove garlic, minced
1 pint button mushrooms, cleaned and sliced
¼ cup cognac
2 teaspoons Dijon mustard
2 teaspoons Worcestershire sauce
½ cup heavy cream
mint jellies, to serve
minced parsley, to garnish

PREPARATION

1. In a cast-iron pan over high heat, warm the olive oil. Season the steak with salt and pepper on both sides. Sear the steak for 2 minutes on each side. Remove from the pan and set aside, covered.
2. In the same pan over medium heat, melt the butter and add the shallot. Cook for 3 to 4 minutes or until soft. Add the garlic and mushrooms. Cook for 4 minutes. Take the pan off the heat and add the cognac. Carefully ignite it with a long match and let the flames die down. Stir in the mustard, Worcestershire sauce, and cream. Season with salt and pepper.
3. Return the steak back to the pan and cook until the internal temperature reaches 125°F for medium-rare, if desired.
4. Serve the steak with the remaining sauce spooned over the top and mint jellies on the side. Garnish with minced parsley.

Aunt Clara's Coq au Vin

AUNT CLARA STEPS IN TO COOK A FRENCH COQ AU VIN so Samantha can make a great impression on her in-laws. This classic dish of chicken braised in red wine with mushrooms and onions is delicious--unless you cast a spell as a shortcut and find a live chicken in the pot instead.

SERVINGS: 4 ✦ PREPARATION TIME: 20 MINS ✦ COOKING TIME: 1 HOUR

INGREDIENTS

4 strips bacon, cut into ½-inch dice
4 chicken thighs, skin-on
salt and pepper, as needed
1 yellow onion, diced small
3 cloves garlic, minced
1 pint button mushrooms, cleaned and sliced
2 carrots, peeled and diced medium
2 tablespoons all-purpose flour
2 tablespoons unsalted butter
2 cups red wine
¼ cup cognac
1 ½ cups chicken stock
2 sprigs thyme
1 bay leaf
minced parsley, to garnish

PREPARATION

1. In a heavy-bottomed pot over medium-high heat, cook the bacon until crisp. Remove from the pot and set aside.
2. Season the chicken on both sides with salt and pepper. In the same pot, sear the chicken thighs, skin-side down, until golden brown, 3 to 4 minutes. Flip and cook the other side for another 3 minutes or until golden. Remove from the pot and set aside.
3. Add the onion and garlic to the pot and cook for 5 minutes or until soft. Add the mushrooms and carrots and cook for 8 to 10 minutes. Season with salt and pepper.
4. Mix in the flour and butter and cook for 1 minute. Add the red wine, cognac, stock, thyme, and bay leaf. Return the chicken and bacon back to the pot. Bring to a boil, then lower the heat to a simmer.
5. Cook for 30 minutes or until the internal temperature of the chicken reaches 165°F. Remove the thyme sprigs and bay leaf. Garnish with minced parsley and serve.

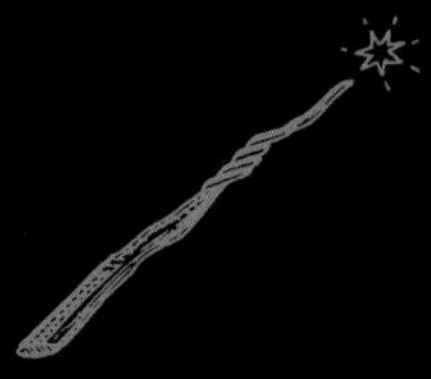

Tournament Bouillabaisse

BOUILLABAISSE IS SERVED DURING THE TRIWIZARD TOURNAMENT when the students of Durmstrang Institute and Beauxbatons Academy of Magic arrive at Hogwarts to compete. Hermione explains to Ron the French origin of this seafood stew that she ate on her summer holiday. Ron, however, is still too skeptical to try a bite.

SERVINGS: 4 ✦ PREPARATION TIME: 30 MINS ✦ COOKING TIME: 30 MINS

INGREDIENTS

¼ cup olive oil
4 tomatoes, coarsely chopped
1 yellow onion, diced small
4 cloves garlic, minced
1 fennel bulb, thinly sliced
1 carrot, peeled and diced medium
1 stalk celery, diced medium
1 bay leaf
pinch of saffron threads
2 sprigs thyme
salt and pepper, as needed
3 cups seafood stock
¼ cup white wine
12 mussels, scrubbed clean
16 small clams, scrubbed clean
1 pound boneless whitefish
minced parsley or basil, to garnish

PREPARATION

1. In a medium pot over medium heat, heat the olive oil. Add the tomatoes, onion, and garlic and cook for 6 minutes or until the onion is soft. Add the fennel, carrot, celery, bay leaf, saffron, and thyme. Cook for another 5 minutes and season with salt and pepper.
2. Pour in the seafood stock and white wine. Bring to a boil, then turn the heat down to a simmer. Add the seafood and cook just until the mussels and clams open.
3. Remove the thyme sprigs and bay leaf. Taste for salt and pepper. Garnish with minced herbs and serve.

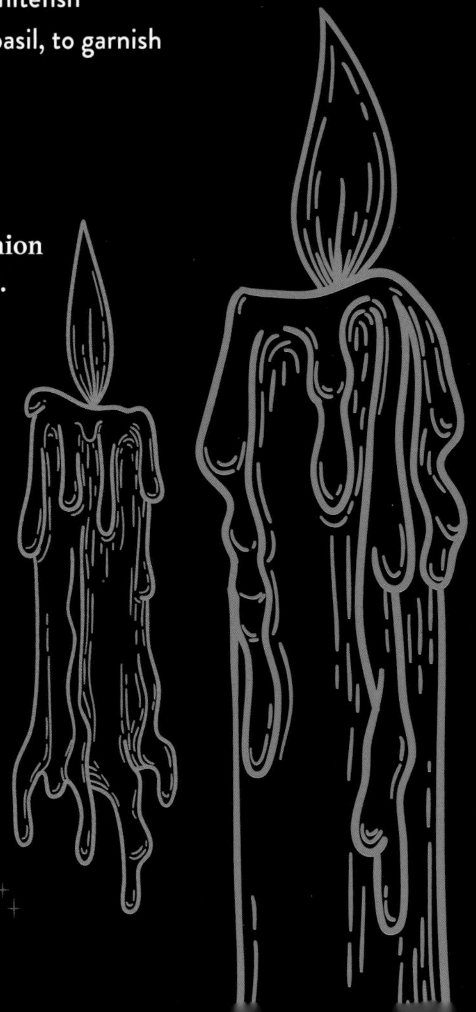

Squash and Herring Pie

ON ONE OF KIKI'S DELIVERY SERVICE ROUTES, she is tasked with helping a grandmother deliver a pie to her granddaughter for her birthday. Though the granddaughter's reaction to their efforts is quite ungrateful, hopefully your guests will appreciate this golden pie that unveils a creamy filling flecked with smoked fish.

SERVINGS: 5 ✦ PREPARATION TIME: 35 MINS ✦ COOKING TIME: 1 HOUR 30 MINS

INGREDIENTS

- 3 pounds butternut squash, peeled and diced large
- 2 tablespoons olive oil
- salt and pepper, as needed
- ½ cup (1 stick) unsalted butter
- 1 leek, cleaned and sliced
- ½ cup all-purpose flour
- 2 cups whole milk
- 1 cup fish stock
- 2 (4.5-ounce) cans smoked herring, drained and torn into bite-size chunks
- all-purpose flour, to dust
- 2 sheets puff pastry
- 1 egg, beaten
- 10 black olives, halved

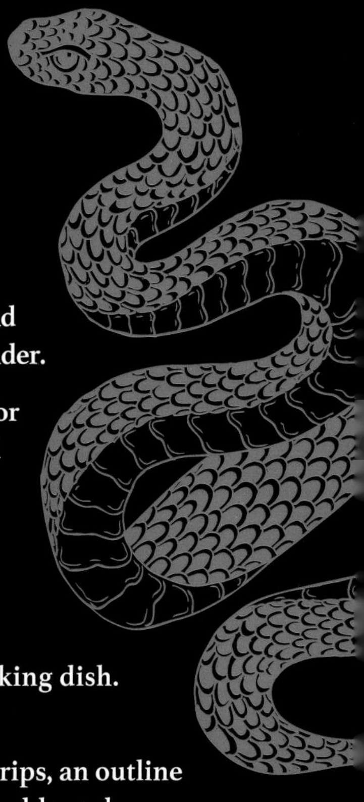

PREPARATION

1. Preheat the oven to 400°F. Line a baking sheet with parchment paper.
2. In a large bowl, toss the butternut squash with the olive oil, salt, and pepper. Spread in a single layer on the prepared baking sheet and roast for 20 minutes or until tender.
3. In a saucepan over medium-high heat, melt the butter. Add the leeks and cook for 8 minutes or until soft. Season with salt and pepper. Add the roasted squash and flour. Stir to coat. Stream in the milk and stock. Let it come to a simmer and thicken. If the mixture is too thick, add a bit more water or stock.
4. Fold in the herring and taste for salt and pepper. Pour the filling into a 9 x 11-inch baking dish and set aside to cool.
5. On a floured surface, roll out a sheet of puff pastry to fit the size of your baking dish. Place it on top of the cooled filling as you work on the next sheet of pastry.
6. Roll out the second sheet of pastry to 9 x 11 inches. Cut out five 1-inch-wide strips, an outline of a fish, five small strips for the body, an eye, and a strip for the mouth. Assemble and adhere the strips and fish to the pastry sheet with the beaten egg. Brush the pastry with the egg and gently press the cut olives onto the sides of the pie.
7. Bake for 45 minutes or until golden brown. Let cool slightly and serve warm.

Chicken à la King

Agnes always makes sure to have a gourmet meal for four on hand in case of emergencies. This decadent and creamy dish of chicken, mushrooms, and pimentos can be served with rice, toast, or pasta. With just a little magic, this dish will come together in a snap!

SERVINGS: 4 ✦ PREPARATION TIME: 10 MINS ✦ COOKING TIME: 20 MINS

INGREDIENTS

4 tablespoons unsalted butter
1 yellow onion, diced
1 pint button mushrooms, cleaned and sliced
3 tablespoons all-purpose flour
¼ cup sherry
1 ½ cups chicken stock
½ cup heavy cream
⅓ cup green peas
1 tablespoon chopped pimento peppers
1 cooked chicken breast, shredded
salt and pepper, as needed
cooked rice, to serve
minced parsley, to garnish

PREPARATION

1. In a skillet over medium-high heat, melt the butter and add the onion. Cook for 5 minutes and then add the mushrooms. Cook for 5 to 6 minutes or until the mushrooms are golden brown.
2. Stir in the flour and cook for 1 minute. While whisking, stream in the sherry, then the chicken stock and heavy cream. Let the mixture simmer until it thickens. Stir in the peas, pimento, and chicken. Simmer for 5 minutes and taste for salt and pepper.
3. Serve with rice and garnish with minced parsley.

Palace Fish and Cabbage Pie

SASHA INTRODUCES VASYA AS HIS BROTHER UPON ENTERING THE PALACE and meeting the Crown Prince, Dmitrii Ivanovich. They are led to a room where the tables are piled with cakes, soup, and platters of food. In the middle is a great pie filled with smoked fish, eggs, and cabbage.

SERVINGS: 6 ✦ PREPARATION TIME: 25 MINS ✦ COOKING TIME: 1 HOUR 10 MINS

INGREDIENTS

- 2 tablespoons unsalted butter
- 1 yellow onion, diced
- ½ head green cabbage, cored and shredded
- 1 tablespoon red wine vinegar
- salt and pepper, as needed
- 1 pound boneless, skinless salmon
- 2 hard-boiled eggs, peeled
- 1 cup cooked brown rice
- 2 eggs, beaten, divided
- ½ cup grated cheddar cheese
- 2 tablespoons chopped dill
- 2 sheets puff pastry

PREPARATION

1. Preheat the oven to 400°F.
2. In a skillet over medium heat, melt the butter and cook the onion for 5 to 6 minutes or until soft. Add the cabbage and vinegar. Season with salt and pepper and cook for 8 minutes, stirring occasionally. Remove from the pan and set aside to cool.
3. Season the salmon with salt and pepper on both sides. In the same pan over medium-high heat, cook the salmon for 4 to 5 minutes on each side or until cooked through. Set aside until cool enough to handle, then flake into large chunks.
4. In a bowl, smash the hard-boiled eggs and combine with the cabbage, cooked rice, salmon, 1 beaten egg, grated cheese, and dill. Season with salt and pepper.
5. Cut both sheets of puff pastry to fit a 9 x 9-inch baking dish. Lay one sheet of pastry on the bottom of the dish and spread the cabbage filling on top. Place the second sheet of pastry on top and brush with the remaining beaten egg.
6. Bake for 35 to 40 minutes or until golden brown.

CHAPTER IV

Desserts, Delights, and Divinations

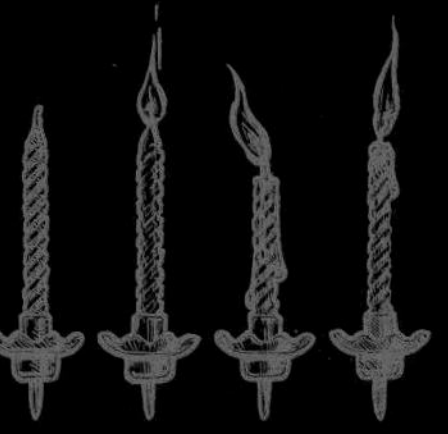

Hilda's Almond Cookies

SHIRLEY JACKSON ENJOYS HILDA'S ALMOND COOKIES as she attempts to tear the sisters apart in order to bring down Zelda as she ascends the ranks in the Church of Night. The plan seems to go accordingly until the hidden cyanide in the cookies and the bitter taste of a failed scheme reveal themselves. Shirley realizes in her last moments never to come between the bond of two sisters.

MAKES: 12 COOKIES ✦ **PREPARATION TIME: 10 MINS** ✦ **COOKING TIME: 20 MINS**

INGREDIENTS

- 1 ½ cups almond flour
- ½ cup all-purpose flour
- ½ cup sugar
- ½ teaspoon baking powder
- ½ teaspoon kosher salt
- 1 egg
- ½ teaspoon vanilla extract
- ½ teaspoon almond extract
- 1 cup almonds, roasted and finely chopped
- 12 whole roasted almonds, for garnish

PREPARATION

1. Preheat the oven to 350°F. Line a baking sheet with parchment paper.
2. In a stand mixer fitted with a paddle attachment, mix the almond flour, all-purpose flour, sugar, baking powder, and salt until well combined.
3. Add the egg, vanilla extract, and almond extract. Mix on low speed just until it comes together.
4. Divide the dough into 12 equal portions. Press each portion into the chopped almonds and flatten it out into a disk. Press a whole almond into the center and repeat with the remaining dough.
5. Bake for 15 minutes or until lightly golden brown.

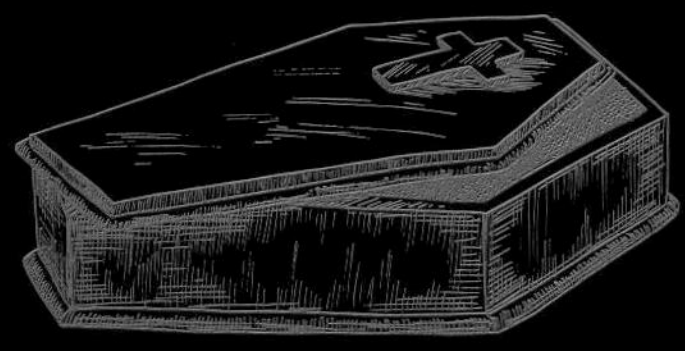

Brownie Pig-Out

THE GLORY DAYS OF HIGH SCHOOL USUALLY BECOME FLEETING MEMORIES AS WE GET OLDER, but for Catherine Madison, the lure to relive her youthful days is too tempting to resist. The power of Catherine's magic and evil scheme reveals itself as Buffy and the gang storm into the Madison household to realize Catherine has cast a spell to switch bodies with her daughter Amy.

MAKES: 16 BROWNIES ✦ PREPARATION TIME: 20 MINS ✦ COOKING TIME: 35 MINS

INGREDIENTS

BROWNIES

- ¾ cup all-purpose flour
- ⅓ cup Dutch-process cocoa powder
- 1 cup (2 sticks) unsalted butter
- 12 ounces dark chocolate, chopped
- 3 eggs, at room temperature
- 1 cup sugar
- 1 tablespoon espresso powder
- 1 tablespoon vanilla extract
- 1 teaspoon kosher salt

MERINGUE

- 3 egg whites
- ¼ teaspoon cream of tartar
- ¼ cup sugar

PREPARATION

1. To make the brownies: Preheat the oven to 350°F. Line an 8-inch square baking dish with parchment paper.
2. In a small bowl, whisk together the flour and cocoa powder. Set aside.
3. Bring a saucepan of water to a simmer over medium heat. Place a bowl over the saucepan and melt the butter and chocolate together until smooth.
4. In the bowl of a stand mixer fitted with a whisk attachment, whisk the eggs and sugar on medium speed until pale yellow. Mix in the espresso powder, vanilla extract, and salt until combined.
5. Stir in the chocolate and butter mixture. Add the flour mixture and mix just until combined.
6. Pour the mixture into the prepared pan and bake for 20 minutes. Let cool before removing from the pan.
7. To make the meringue: Place the egg whites in a clean mixing bowl of a stand mixer fitted with a whisk attachment. Whisk on medium speed until foamy. Add the cream of tartar and mix until the egg whites begin to hold their shape. Slowly stream in the sugar and mix until the mixture holds a stiff peak.
8. Spread the meringue on top of the brownie. Use a kitchen torch to toast the meringue until golden brown. Alternatively, place under the broiler, watching carefully. Cut into squares to serve.

Mrs. Cole Turner's Apple Pie

I HAVE BAKED MY HUSBAND THE MOST PERFECT APPLE PIE, and I know he will be delighted to eat it for dessert tonight. I must clean up the house after those pesky demonic bounty hunters have completely destroyed the place!

SERVINGS: 6–8 ✦ PREPARATION TIME: 20 MINS ✦ COOKING TIME: 2 HOURS

INGREDIENTS

FILLING

- 2 cups apple cider
- 6 pounds Honeycrisp apples, peeled, cored, and sliced
- 3 tablespoons unsalted butter
- 2 tablespoons lemon juice
- ½ cup all-purpose flour
- ½ cup sugar
- 1 teaspoon ground cinnamon
- 1 teaspoon kosher salt
- 1 teaspoon vanilla extract

CRUST

- 2 ¾ cups all-purpose flour
- 1 teaspoon kosher salt
- 1 cup (2 sticks) unsalted butter, thinly sliced and frozen cold
- ½ cup ice-cold water
- 1 egg, beaten

PREPARATION

1. To begin the filling: Bring the apple cider to a simmer in a small saucepan over medium heat. Simmer gently until it reduces to ¼ cup of thick liquid. This will take about 45 minutes. Set aside.
2. To make the crust: In the bowl of a stand mixer fitted with a paddle attachment, mix the flour and salt. Add the butter and mix on low speed until the butter pieces are about the size of walnut halves. Stream in the ice water just until the dough comes together when pressed. Divide the dough into two disks. Wrap with plastic and refrigerate for 30 minutes.
3. To finish the filling: In a heavy-bottomed pot, combine the apples, butter, lemon juice, flour, sugar, cinnamon, and salt. Cook over medium heat for 5 to 6 minutes or until the apples are soft and tender. Stir in the reduced apple cider and vanilla and set aside to cool.
4. Preheat the oven to 400°F. Roll out both disks of pie dough until they are about ¼-inch thick and 12 inches in diameter. Press one crust gently into the pie dish and then fill with the cooled apple filling.
5. Cut the second crust into ½- to ¾-inch-wide strips. Lay out six or seven parallel strips on top of the apple filling. Fold back every other strip and place another long strip perpendicular to the first strips. Unfold the strips, then repeat the same steps with the other strips. Keep alternating until complete. Trim the excess dough or crimp the edges.
6. Brush the crust with the beaten egg and bake for 1 hour or until golden brown.

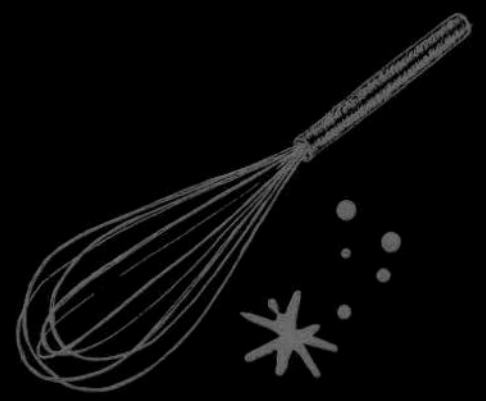

Pineapple Upside-Down Cake

I WOULDN'T BE THE PERFECT HOUSEWIFE if I didn't have the perfect dessert ready to top off the night! This pineapple upside-down cake is just what my neighbor, Wanda, needs to finish off the perfect gourmet dinner to impress her husband's boss. There's never been a little chaos I couldn't handle!

SERVINGS: 6 ✦ PREPARATION TIME: 20 MINS ✦ COOKING TIME: 1 HOUR

INGREDIENTS

- 4 tablespoons unsalted butter, at room temperature
- ½ cup dark brown sugar
- 7 pineapple rings
- 4 maraschino cherries, halved and patted dry
- 1 ½ cups all-purpose flour
- ½ cup cornmeal
- 1 teaspoon baking soda
- ½ teaspoon salt
- 1 cup buttermilk
- 2 eggs
- ¾ cup granulated sugar
- 1 teaspoon vanilla extract
- 4 tablespoons unsalted butter, melted and cooled
- ¼ cup turbinado sugar

PREPARATION

1. Preheat the oven to 350°F. Coat the bottom of an 8-inch round cake pan with the softened butter. Spread the dark brown sugar evenly on the bottom of the pan. Place the pineapple rings on top of the brown sugar in a single layer. Place the halved cherries in the center of each pineapple. Set the pan aside.
2. In the bowl of a stand mixer fitted with a paddle attachment, mix the flour, cornmeal, baking soda, and salt.
3. On medium speed, add the buttermilk, eggs, granulated sugar, vanilla, and melted butter. Mix until well combined. Pour the batter into the prepared pan and bake for 50 to 55 minutes, until a toothpick comes out clean when inserted into the center.
4. Let cool for 5 to 10 minutes. Carefully invert the cake onto a serving platter. To serve, spread an even layer of turbinado sugar on top and use a torch to caramelize the sugar. Slice and serve.

ANNE'S PEACH PIE

WHEN BUFFY RUNS AWAY TO LOS ANGELES, she finds a job as a waitress in a quiet diner and goes by the name of Anne. During one of her shifts, Buffy recommends the peach pie to a pair of diners who had recently gotten matching tattoos. Though she quietly mentions that there might not be any actual peaches in it, the comment goes unnoticed by the couple, who quickly return to their conversation about the troubles of their current situation.

SERVINGS: 6–8 ✦ **PREPARATION TIME: 30 MINS** ✦ **COOKING TIME: 1 HOUR**

INGREDIENTS

CRUST

2 ¾ cups all-purpose flour

1 teaspoon kosher salt

1 cup (2 sticks) unsalted butter, thinly sliced and frozen cold

½ cup ice-cold water

FILLING

9 large yellow peaches, pitted and sliced into wedges

¾ cup granulated sugar

½ cup all-purpose flour

1 teaspoon vanilla extract

1 egg, beaten

2 tablespoons turbinado sugar

PREPARATION

1. To make the crust: In the bowl of stand mixer fitted with a paddle attachment, combine the flour and salt. Add the butter and mix on low speed until the butter pieces are about the size of walnut halves. Stream in the ice water just until the dough comes together when pressed. Divide the dough into two disks. Wrap with plastic and refrigerate for 30 minutes.
2. To make the filling: In a bowl, mix together the peaches, granulated sugar, flour, and vanilla.
3. Preheat the oven to 400°F.
4. Roll out both pieces of dough until they're ¼ inch thick and 1 inch wider than an 11-inch pie dish. Gently press one crust into the pie dish and fill with the peach filling. Place the second pie crust on top and tuck the overhang to create a clean edge. Crimp and seal the edges as desired.
5. Brush the top with the beaten egg and sprinkle with the turbinado sugar. Cut four slits on the top for ventilation.
6. Bake for 55 minutes to 1 hour or until golden brown. Let cool before serving.

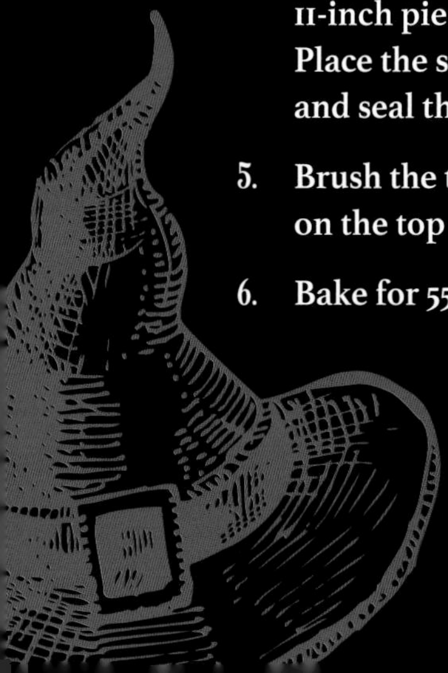

Juicy Sweet Caramel Apple

Today is Free Caramel Apple Day! Try our juicy sweet apple covered with salted caramel and a very secret ingredient. Come on, take a bite!

SERVINGS: 4 ✦ PREPARATION TIME: 8 MINS ✦ COOKING TIME: 10 MINS

INGREDIENTS

- 1 (11-ounce) bag of caramels, unwrapped
- ½ teaspoon kosher salt
- Black food coloring, as needed
- 4 wooden skewers
- 4 medium Granny Smith apples
- 1 (0.43-ounce) pack green apple flavor Fun Dip
- Chunky gold sprinkles, as needed

PREPARATION

1. Melt the caramels and salt in a double boiler over medium heat. Stir occasionally to help the caramels melt evenly. Once melted, add 2 or 3 drops of black food coloring. Add more if needed to achieve the desired color. Stir to combine.
2. Stick a skewer into each apple and dip in the warm caramel to coat. Tap off the excess and immediately coat the bottom with the gold sprinkles.
3. Sprinkle a bit of green apple Fun Dip powder on top.
4. Repeat with the remaining apples.

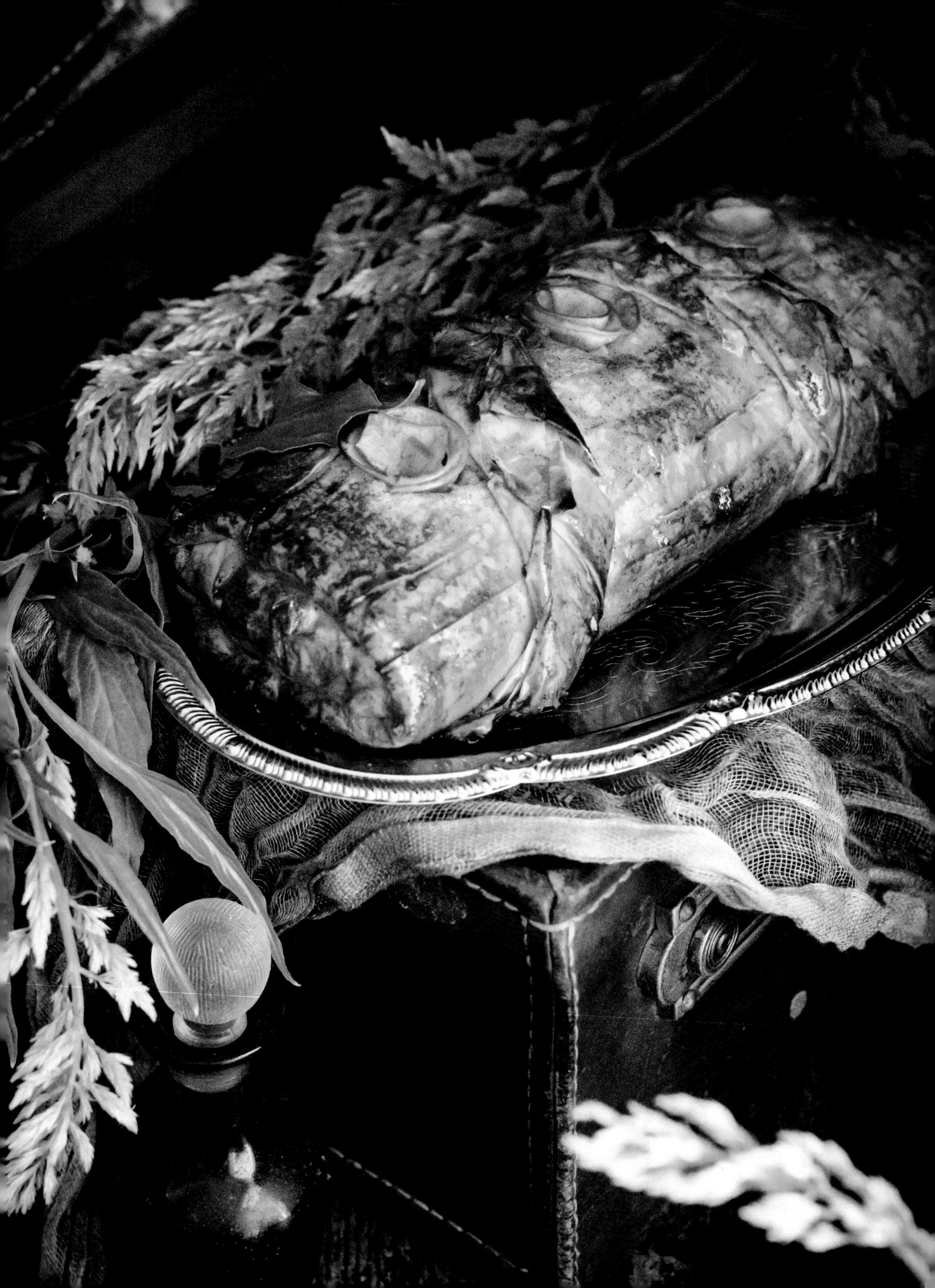

Magical Apple Strudel

Enchant your dinner guests with a Magical Apple Strudel for dessert. Layers of flaky and buttery pastry unveil the most tender and delicious apple filling. This will make everyone believe in magic.

SERVINGS: 4–6 ✦ **PREPARATION TIME: 30 MINS** ✦ **COOKING TIME: 50 MINS**

✶ INGREDIENTS

- 3 or 4 medium Golden Delicious apples, peeled, cored, and cut into ½-inch dice
- ½ cup golden raisins
- ½ cup granulated sugar
- ½ teaspoon ground cinnamon
- ¼ teaspoon kosher salt
- ½ cup chopped walnuts
- 7 phyllo layers
- ½ cup (1 stick) unsalted butter, melted
- ¼ cup panko breadcrumbs

✶ PREPARATION

1. Preheat the oven to 375°F. Line a baking sheet with parchment paper.
2. In a bowl, mix together the apples, raisins, granulated sugar, cinnamon, and salt. Pour the mixture into a saucepan over medium heat and cook for 15 to 20 minutes or until the juices have evaporated and the apples have softened. Stir in the chopped walnuts and set aside to cool to room temperature.
3. Unroll the phyllo dough on your work surface. Keep it covered with plastic wrap while you work to prevent it from drying out. Brush one sheet of phyllo with melted butter and dust with powdered sugar. Repeat with the remaining sheets, layering them on top of each other as you go.
4. Working along the length of the phyllo layers, spread the breadcrumbs on the phyllo, leaving a 2-inch border. Place the apple filling on top.
5. Fold in the ends, then roll in from the long edge to create a log. Brush the outside with the remaining butter. Transfer the strudel to the prepared baking sheet.
6. With any remaining phyllo dough, you can create flowers or a braid to go along the strudel.
7. Cut three slits on the top and adorn the strudel as desired.
8. Bake for 30 minutes or until golden brown. Let cool for a few minutes before serving.

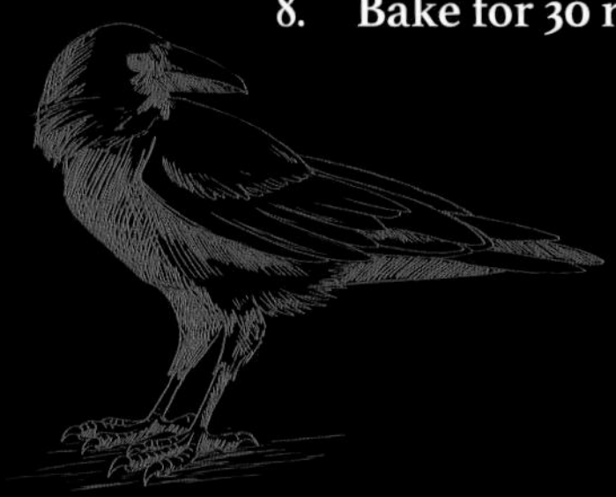

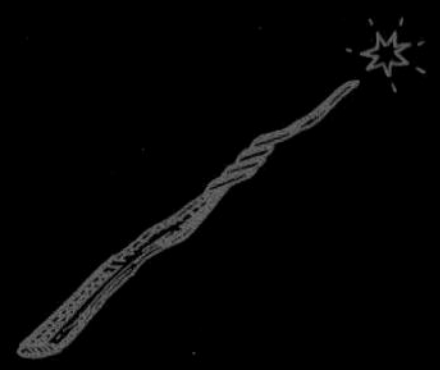

Ginger Newt Biscuits

Ginger newt biscuits are a favorite treat of Professor McGonagall. Typically held in a tartan box on her desk, these nutty and gingery biscuits are perfect with an afternoon cup of tea. Don't let these little treats slither away before you've had a chance to try them!

MAKES: 12 BISCUITS ✦ PREPARATION TIME: 10 MINS ✦ COOKING TIME: 10 MINS

INGREDIENTS

- ½ cup almond butter
- ⅓ cup finely chopped almonds
- ¼ cup golden syrup
- ½ teaspoon kosher salt
- ½ teaspoon ground cinnamon
- ¼ teaspoon baking soda
- ⅓ cup currants
- ½ cup rolled oats
- 2 tablespoons finely chopped candied ginger
- 1 egg, beaten

PREPARATION

1. Preheat the oven to 350°F. Line a baking sheet with parchment paper.
2. In a bowl, mix together all the ingredients until well combined. Press the mixture between two sheets of parchment paper and roll it out until it is ½ inch thick.
3. Cut out biscuits using a newt-shaped cookie cutter. Use a toothpick to release the more delicate areas around the legs and neck. Place on the prepared baking sheet and refrigerate for 15 minutes.
4. Bake for 10 minutes or until golden brown.

White Witch's Turkish Delight

LURED BY THE COMFORT OF THE WITCH AND HER ENCHANTED DISH OF TURKISH DELIGHT, Edmund Pevensie is quick to betray his family for the promise of power and more of this delightful confection. Coated in powdered sugar and flecked with chopped pistachios, this marvelous treat might turn the closest of siblings against each other just for a bite.

SERVINGS: 8–10 ✦ PREPARATION TIME: 20 MINS ✦ COOKING TIME: 2 HOURS
SET TIME: 4 HOURS OR OVERNIGHT

✶ INGREDIENTS

3 ½ cups water, divided
1 tablespoon lemon juice
3 cups granulated sugar
1 cup cornstarch
1 teaspoon cream of tartar
1 tablespoon rose water
4 or 5 drops red food coloring
¼ cup chopped pistachios
1 cup powdered sugar

✶ PREPARATION

1. Line an 8 x 8-inch baking pan with parchment paper to cover the bottom and two sides of the pan. Generously grease the pan and the parchment paper with oil and set aside.
2. In a large saucepan over medium-high heat, combine 1 ½ cups of the water, lemon juice, and granulated sugar and bring to a boil. Using a candy thermometer, let the syrup simmer until it reaches 240°F. This should take around 20 minutes. Try not to stir too much to prevent the sugar from crystallizing.
3. In another saucepan over medium heat, whisk together the cornstarch, cream of tartar, and remaining 2 cups of water. Cook until it turns into a smooth white paste. Keep stirring and whisking the mixture to ensure no lumps form.
4. Once the sugar reaches 240°F, stream the syrup into the cornstarch mixture a bit at a time. Whisk to incorporate after each addition. Return the pot back to medium heat and let it cook for 45 to 50 minutes, stirring occasionally. The mixture should be thick, glossy, and golden in color.
5. Stir in the rose water, food coloring, and chopped nuts. Scoop the mixture into the prepared pan and spread it out evenly with an offset spatula. Cover with plastic wrap and let it cool and set until firm enough to cut, approximately 4 hours or overnight.
6. Remove the Turkish delight from the pan and cut into bite-size pieces with an oiled knife. Coat each piece generously with powdered sugar.

Marthe's Special Cake

MARTHE IS A KNOWN TALENT IN THE KITCHEN. For Margaret's ceremony, she creates a special cake topped with strands of sugar. The cotton candy gives this dessert the instant touch of magic and whimsy that might resemble what comes out of Marthe's kitchen.

SERVINGS: 8 ✦ PREPARATION TIME: 20 MINS ✦ COOKING TIME: 1 HOUR

INGREDIENTS

CAKE

1 ½ cups all-purpose flour
1 ½ teaspoons baking powder
½ teaspoon kosher salt
1 tablespoon lemon zest
⅓ cup sugar
½ cup currants
½ cup (1 stick) cold unsalted butter, diced
½ cup whole milk

CUSTARD

4 egg yolks
¼ cup sugar
2 teaspoons cornstarch
2 cups whole milk
1 vanilla bean, split
Cotton candy, to garnish

PREPARATION

1. Preheat the oven to 400°F. Grease 8 small ramekins with the softened butter and set aside.
2. To make the cake: In a large bowl, mix together the flour, baking powder, salt, lemon zest, sugar, and currants. Cut in the cold butter with a pastry blender and incorporate until the butter pieces are the size of green peas. Stream in the milk and mix together just until combined.
3. Divide the batter equally among the ramekins and place them into a deep baking dish. Pour enough boiling water into the dish until it reaches three-fourths of the way up the sides of the ramekins. Cover with foil and bake for 30 minutes.
4. To make the custard: In a medium bowl, whisk together the egg yolks, sugar, and cornstarch until smooth.
5. In a saucepan over medium-high heat, combine the milk and vanilla bean and bring just to a simmer. Remove from the heat and carefully stream it into the yolk mixture, whisking constantly.
6. Pour the mixture back into the saucepan. Over medium-low heat, continue to cook and whisk as the custard thickens. The custard is ready when it sticks to the back of a spoon and leaves a path when you draw your finger across.
7. Invert the cakes onto a serving plate and serve with the warm custard. Garnish with cotton candy.

The Poisonous Apple

WHO IS THE FAIREST ONE OF ALL? These *choux au craquelin*, filled with tender apples and vanilla cream.

MAKES: 12 PASTRIES ✦ PREPARATION TIME: 1 HOUR 30 MINS ✦ COOKING TIME: 1 HOUR

INGREDIENTS

CRAQUELIN
½ cup brown sugar
½ cup (1 stick) unsalted butter, at room temperature
1 scant cup all-purpose flour
½ teaspoon vanilla extract
3 or 4 drops red gel food coloring

CHOUX PASTRY
1 cup water
1 cup whole milk
1 cup (2 sticks) unsalted butter
2 ½ cups all-purpose flour
3 tablespoons granulated sugar
1 teaspoon kosher salt
8 eggs, beaten

APPLE FILLING
2 apples, peeled, cored, and diced medium
¼ cup dark brown sugar
1 tablespoon lemon juice
½ teaspoon ground cinnamon

2 cups fresh whipped cream

PREPARATION

1. Preheat the oven to 375°F. Line two baking sheets with parchment paper.
2. To make the craquelin: In a bowl of stand mixer fitted with a paddle attachment, mix together the craquelin ingredients. Place the mixture between two sheets of parchment paper and roll it out until it is ¼-inch thick. Refrigerate for 30 minutes. With a cookie cutter, cut out 12 circles 2 ½ inches or large enough to cover your pastries. Place on one of the prepared baking sheets and keep cold.
3. To make the choux pastry: In a saucepan over medium-high heat, combine the water, milk, and butter. Bring the mixture to a boil and immediately add the flour, granulated sugar, and salt. Stir to combine and lower the heat to medium-low. Cook for 6 minutes, stirring constantly. Transfer the choux pastry to the mixer and mix on medium speed for 1 to 2 minutes. Slowly stream in the beaten eggs until the batter webs around the paddle and bowl.
4. Scoop out 12 portions of the batter onto the second baking sheet. Top each with craquelin and bake for 35 minutes.
5. To make the filling: In a saucepan over medium heat, combine the apples, brown sugar, lemon juice, and cinnamon and cook for 15 minutes or until the apples are tender.
6. To assemble, slice the tops off the choux pastries and fill with 1 to 2 tablespoons of the apple filling. Spoon on whipped cream and top with the lid.

Spell Cake to Change Your Fate

LED THROUGH THE FOREST TO A COTTAGE WHERE AN OLD WITCH AND HER CROW LIVE, Merida asks the witch for a spell that will change her fate. After the witch tosses a few ingredients into her cauldron, a bright light flashes through the cottage, and a pastry dusted with powdered sugar emerges from the bubbling concoction. Inside the pastry are layers of wild blueberry jam and sweet almond paste held together by a golden crust.

SERVINGS: 4 ✦ PREPARATION TIME: 35 MINS ✦ COOKING TIME: 45 MINS

INGREDIENTS

CRUST

1 ½ cups all-purpose flour
2 tablespoons granulated sugar
½ teaspoon kosher salt
¾ cup (1 ½ sticks) cold unsalted butter, diced
1 egg, beaten

FILLING

4 tablespoons unsalted butter, at room temperature
¼ cup granulated sugar
½ cup almond flour
1 egg
1 tablespoon all-purpose flour
blueberry jam, as needed
1 egg, beaten
powdered sugar, as needed

PREPARATION

1. To make the crust: In the bowl of a stand mixer fitted with a paddle attachment, combine the flour, granulated sugar, and salt. Add the cold butter and beaten egg and mix just until the dough starts to come together. Form into a disk, wrap with plastic wrap, and refrigerate for 30 minutes.
2. To make the filling: While the dough is chilling, in a bowl, mix together the softened butter, granulated sugar, almond flour, egg, and all-purpose flour until well combined. Set aside.
3. Preheat the oven to 375°F.
4. On a floured surface, roll the dough to ⅛-inch thickness. Cut out a 7 ½-inch-wide circle to fit the base of a mini pie or cake pan. Cut out another circle 6 inches in diameter. Press the larger circle into the pan and trim off any extra pastry with a sharp knife. With the extra dough, cut out three strips to create braids for the edges of the pastry.
5. On the bottom of the pastry, spread 3 tablespoons of blueberry jam and top it with the almond mixture. Brush the edges with the beaten egg and place the smaller circle of pastry on top. Place the braided dough around the edge. Brush with the beaten egg and refrigerate for 10 minutes.
6. Transfer to the oven and bake for 30 to 35 minutes or until golden brown. Let cool and dust with powdered sugar. Cut a circle in the center and fill with more blueberry jam.

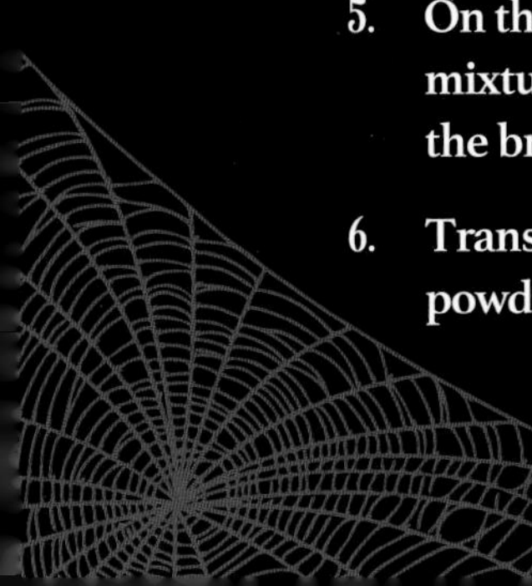

Grams's Chocolate Cake

Both talented in the kitchen, Piper and Grams have always bonded over cooking and baking. When Prue eats all the brownies, Grams and Piper make double chocolate decadence cake together.

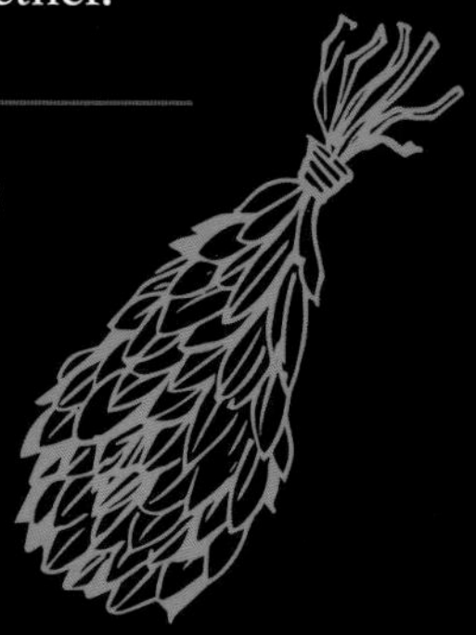

SERVINGS: 8 ✦ PREPARATION TIME: 40 MINS ✦ COOKING TIME: 1 HOUR

INGREDIENTS

CAKE

⅓ cup hot water
½ cup unsweetened cocoa powder
⅓ cup whole milk
1 ¼ cups all-purpose flour
1 tablespoon espresso powder
½ teaspoon baking soda
½ teaspoon kosher salt
¾ cup (1 ½ sticks) unsalted butter, at room temperature
1 ½ cups sugar
2 eggs, at room temperature

FROSTING

1 cup heavy cream
8 ounces chopped dark chocolate
½ cup sour cream

chocolate shavings, to garnish

PREPARATION

1. Preheat the oven to 350°F and butter two 7-inch round cake pans. Dust with cocoa powder and tap out the excess. Set aside. To make the cake: In a bowl, whisk together the hot water and cocoa powder until smooth. Stream in the milk and set aside.
2. In another bowl, mix the flour, espresso powder, baking soda, and salt.
3. In the bowl of a stand mixer fitted with a paddle attachment, cream together the butter and sugar until light and smooth. Add the eggs and mix on medium speed until well combined. Alternate adding the dry ingredients and the cocoa mixture in two or three additions.
4. Divide the batter equally between the two prepared pans and bake for 40 minutes . Cool for 10 minutes, then invert the cakes onto a cooling rack.
5. To make the frosting: In a saucepan over medium heat, add the cream and bring it just to a simmer. Place the chopped chocolate in a bowl, pour over the hot cream, and let it sit for 3 to 4 minutes. Stir to incorporate. Once smooth, stir in the sour cream and set aside to cool and thicken.
6. To assemble the cake, place a cake layer on a cake stand or plate, spread the frosting on top, and top with the second cake. Spread the remaining frosting on the top and sides of the cake, if desired. Garnish with chocolate shavings.

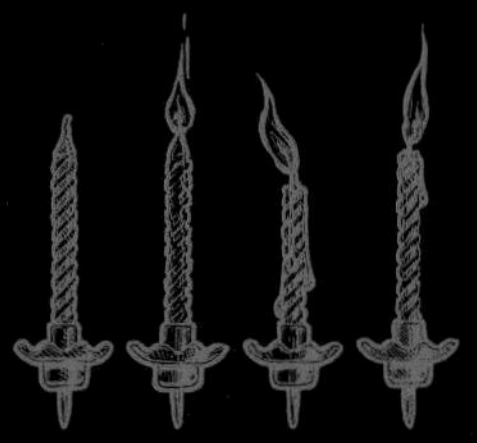

Aunt Hilda's Truth Cake

AUNT HILDA'S ELABORATE CONFECTION OF MARCHPANE, brandied currants, and brown butter cake is truly a sight to behold. Just one bite of this cake will make it impossible for anyone to lie.

SERVINGS: 8–10 ✦ PREPARATION TIME: 2 HOURS ✦ COOKING TIME: 1 HOUR

INGREDIENTS

CAKE

1 scant cup all-purpose flour
1 ⅓ cups almond flour
2 ½ cups powdered sugar
1 teaspoon kosher salt
10 ½ ounces egg whites
10 ½ ounces brown butter, melted and cooled

FROSTING

1 cup currants
½ cup hot water
¼ cup brandy
1 cup (2 sticks) unsalted butter
½ teaspoon vanilla extract
3 cups powdered sugar, sifted
1 tablespoon whole milk

TO DECORATE

4 ounces marzipan
27 ounces navy blue fondant
3 ounces white fondant
edible gold luster dust, as needed
vodka, as needed

PREPARATION

1. Preheat the oven to 350°F and line two 7-inch round cake pans with parchment paper. To make the cake: In the bowl of a stand mixer fitted with a paddle attachment, mix the two flours, powdered sugar, and salt until combined. Stream in the egg whites and mix on medium speed until well combined. Stream in the brown butter. Pour the batter equally between the prepared pans and bake for 45 minutes. Cool for 10 minutes, then invert the cakes onto a cooling rack.

2. To make the frosting: In a small bowl, cover the currants with the hot water and brandy and let sit for 20 to 30 minutes or until soft. Drain the currants and set aside. In the bowl of a stand mixer fitted with a paddle attachment, cream the butter and vanilla until smooth. Add the powdered sugar and mix on medium speed until incorporated. Mix in the milk and currants.

3. To decorate the cake: Divide the marzipan into two balls. In between two sheets of parchment paper, roll out each portion of marzipan into 7-inch circles. Set aside. Spread the frosting on top of the cake layers followed by a layer of marzipan. Frost the surface of the cake and refrigerate for 30 minutes.

4. Combine the navy blue and white fondants and roll it out until it is ¼-inch thick. Drape and ease the fondant over the cake to create a smooth layer, adding ruffles with the excess fondant and drops of water. Mix the edible gold luster dust with a few drops of vodka. Brush on accents.

Knickerbocker Glory

WHEN THE DURSLEYS GO TO THE ZOO TO CELEBRATE DUDLEY'S BIRTHDAY, they experience the great atrocity of a knickerbocker glory with not enough ice cream. While Harry gets to enjoy the leftovers of what Dudley doesn't bother to finish, Vernon orders Dudley another glass to make sure his special day is perfect. This version of knickerbocker glory has a slight twist on the classic with the tartness of the sour cherry jam to accompany the creamy ice cream and toasted vanilla meringue on top.

SERVINGS: 2 ✦ PREPARATION TIME: 15 MINS

INGREDIENTS

MERINGUE

2 egg whites
⅛ teaspoon cream of tartar
5 tablespoons sugar
½ teaspoon vanilla extract

TO ASSEMBLE

¼ cup sour cherry jam
4 scoops vanilla ice cream
1 (8-ounce) can fruit cocktail
2 maraschino cherries
2 rolled wafer cookies

PREPARATION

1. To make the meringue: In the bowl of stand mixer, whip the egg whites on medium speed until frothy. Add the cream of tartar and sugar. Keep whisking until you achieve firm peaks. Add the vanilla and mix to combine.
2. To assemble: Spread the sour cherry jam along the sides of two tall chilled glasses. Layer the ice cream, fruit cocktail, and more jam until you reach the top of the glass. Mound the meringue on top and use a torch to toast the meringue until golden brown. Top each with a cherry and a rolled wafer cookie.

CHAPTER V

Beldam Brews and Beverages

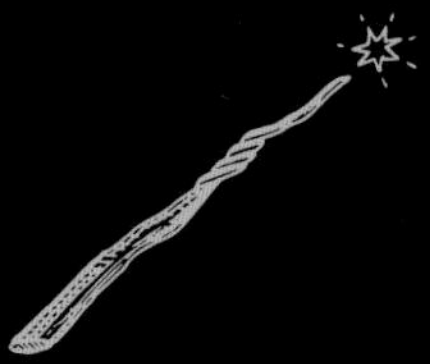

Butterbeer

A TRIP TO HOGSMEADE IS NOT COMPLETE until you and your mates order and enjoy a few tankards of butterbeer at the Three Broomsticks Inn.

SERVINGS: 4 ✦ PREPARATION TIME: 10 MINS ✦ COOKING TIME: 10 MINS

INGREDIENTS

- ½ cup (1 stick) unsalted butter
- ½ cup dark brown sugar
- ½ teaspoon kosher salt
- 1 cup heavy cream
- 1 teaspoon vanilla extract
- 1 teaspoon butter extract
- cream soda, to serve
- whipped cream, to serve

PREPARATION

1. In a saucepan over medium heat, melt the butter, brown sugar, and salt. Bring the mixture to a gentle simmer, stirring occasionally to ensure the bottom doesn't burn. Pour in the heavy cream and stir until well combined.
2. Remove from the heat and stir in the vanilla and butter extract. Set aside to cool.
3. To serve the drink, pour 3 to 4 tablespoons of the butterscotch mixture into a mug and top off with cream soda. Top with whipped cream and a drizzle of the butterscotch.

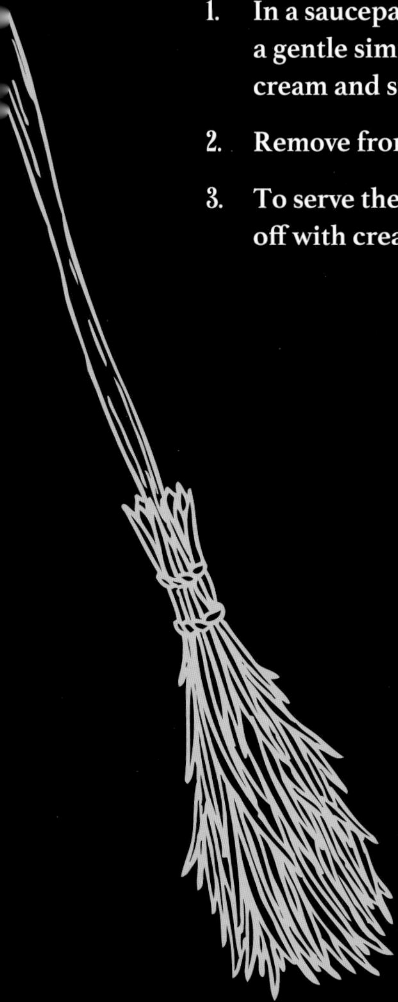

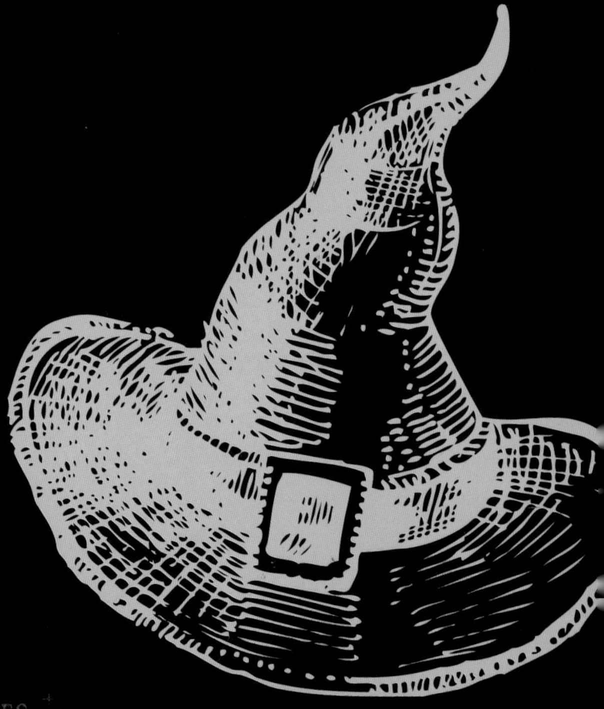

A DISCOVERY OF WITCHES: ALL SOULS TRILOGY

A Weaver's Chai

UPON DIANA BISHOP'S RETURN HOME, Fernando and Amira strike up a conversation about the time they traveled together. On their way to Gharapuri, they had stopped to eat at a stall that served chai made with coconut milk. This comforting drink is a warm mix of spices further enhanced by the richness of coconut milk. Serve this in a large mug or share with a friend.

SERVINGS: 2 ✦ PREPARATION TIME: 5 MINS ✦ COOKING TIME: 15 MINS

INGREDIENTS

2 cups water
2 tablespoons Assam tea
4 cloves
2 cinnamon sticks
4 slices fresh ginger
5 cardamon pods
1 teaspoon black peppercorns
1 cup coconut milk
3 tablespoons sugar or more to taste

PREPARATION

1. Pour the water into a saucepan and bring to a boil. Add the tea, cloves, cinnamon, ginger, cardamon pods, and peppercorns. Lower the heat to a simmer and cook for 5 to 8 minutes.
2. Add the coconut milk and sugar and simmer gently for 5 minutes.
3. Strain out the solids, taste and adjust the sweetness, and serve warm.

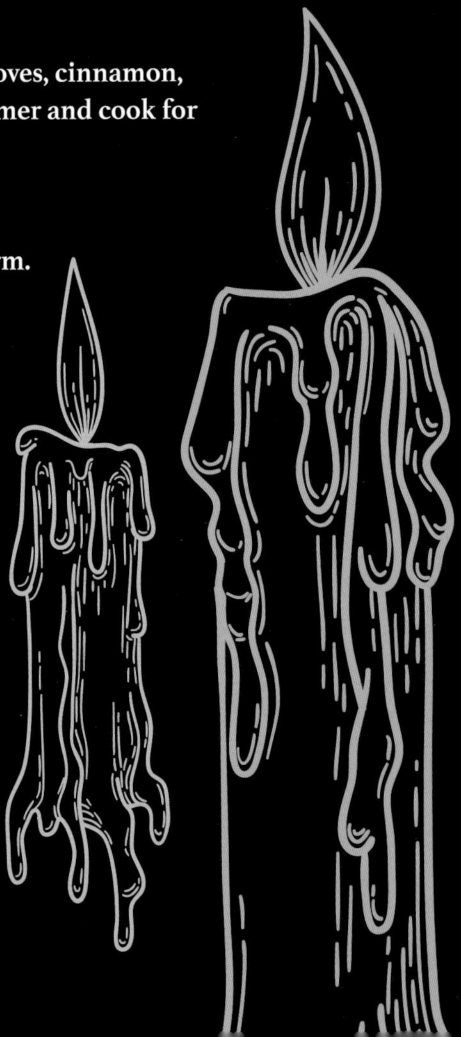

CAUDLE FOR PAINS IN THE HEAD

DIANA ATTEMPTS TO SETTLE INTO HER NEW LIFE after time traveling back to Elizabethan London. Journaling about all her new experiences, she tries to understand the recipe for a caudle she learned from their cook, Charles. While Diana's resulting drink leaves much to be desired, this brew is simple and gives us a peek into what a remedy for a headache might have been like back in sixteenth-century England.

SERVINGS: 2 ✦ **PREPARATION TIME: 5 MINS** ✦ **COOKING TIME: 15 MINS**

INGREDIENTS

- 2 egg yolks, beaten
- 1 ½ cups white wine
- 2 to 3 tablespoons honey, to taste
- 1 pinch of saffron

PREPARATION

1. In a bowl, whisk together the egg yolks, wine, honey, and saffron.
2. Set the bowl over a double boiler of simmering water and cook, stirring, until the mixture warms up and thickens, 8 to 10 minutes.
3. Serve warm.

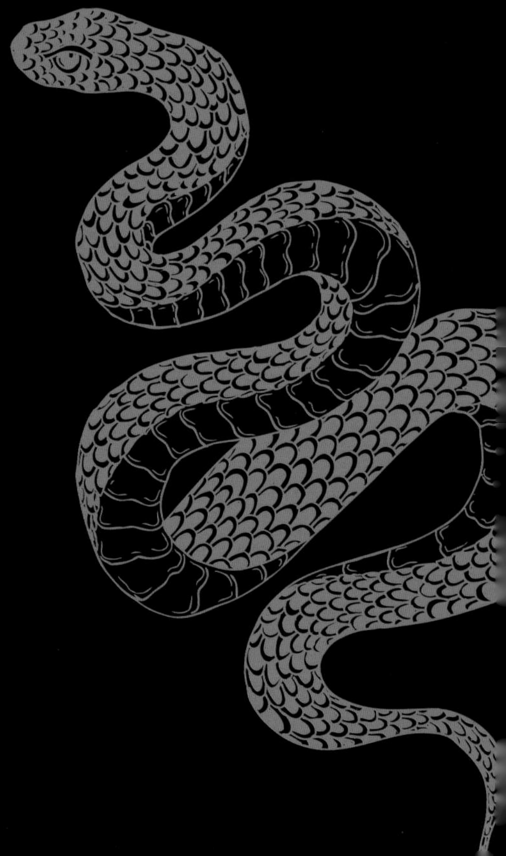

Landon's Peanut Butter Blast

THIS PEANUT BUTTER BLAST WITH WHIPPED CREAM ON THE BOTTOM was exactly what Landon used to serve Hope when he worked at the Mystic Grill. Make this for a special friend.

SERVINGS: 2 ✦ PREPARATION TIME: 5 MINS

INGREDIENTS

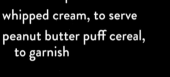

- 1 square white chocolate, melted
- ½ cup crushed Reese's Pieces
- ½ cup whole milk
- ⅓ cup creamy peanut butter
- 3 or 4 scoops vanilla ice cream
- whipped cream, to serve
- peanut butter puff cereal, to garnish

PREPARATION

1. Dip the rim of two milkshake glasses in the melted white chocolate and roll in the crushed Reese's Pieces. Refrigerate until needed.
2. In a blender, combine the milk, peanut butter, and ice cream. Blend until smooth.
3. Spoon the whipped cream into the bottom of the glasses. Pour the milkshake on top and garnish with the peanut butter puff cereal.

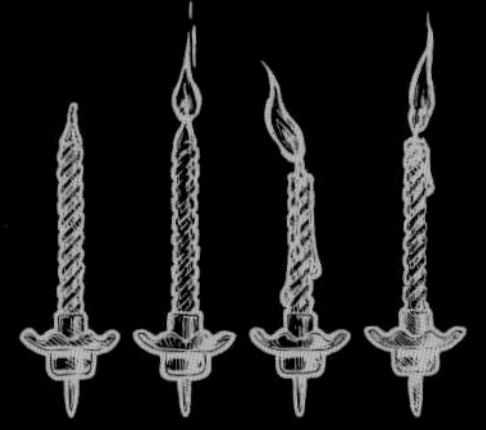

Mr. Kinkle's Eggnog

In an effort to help Harvey and his father, Sabrina brews a special alcohol-free eggnog for Mr. Kinkle. Using Aunt Hilda's secret recipe, Sabrina offers the enchanted drink to Mr. Kinkle so that he will never touch alcohol again. This concoction needs no enchantment, as everyone can enjoy a cup of this sweet and spiced drink during the holidays.

SERVINGS: 4 ✦ PREPARATION TIME: 8 MINS ✦ COOKING TIME: 20 MINS

INGREDIENTS

5 egg yolks
½ cup sugar
½ teaspoon kosher salt
½ cup heavy cream
2 cups whole milk, plus more as needed
2 cinnamon sticks
½ teaspoon vanilla extract
¼ teaspoon grated nutmeg
whipped cream, to serve
ground cinnamon, to garnish

PREPARATION

1. In a bowl, whisk together the egg yolks, sugar, and salt.
2. In a saucepan over medium heat, bring the heavy cream, milk, and cinnamon to a simmer. While whisking, stream the hot cream mixture into the egg yolk mixture. Return the mixture back to the pot.
3. Cook over medium-low heat, stirring constantly, until the mixture has thickened and reaches 160°F. Strain through a fine-mesh colander to remove the cinnamon sticks and any cooked bits of egg. Add the vanilla and nutmeg and stir to combine.
4. Cover and refrigerate until cold.
5. To serve, adjust the consistency with milk if you like it thinner. Serve with whipped cream and a dash of cinnamon.

The Halloween Spirit

ALISON AND HER FAMILY TAKE HALLOWEEN VERY SERIOUSLY. As Max and Dani enter their home on Halloween night, their colonial-themed party is in full swing as Alison offers them cider from a large punch bowl. The bubbly ginger beer brings all the familiar fall flavors of cinnamon and apples in the cider to another level.

SERVINGS: 2–3 ✦ PREPARATION TIME: 10 MINS

INGREDIENTS

2 cups apple cider
1 cup ginger beer
juice of 1 orange
1 cinnamon stick
ice cubes
sliced apples, to garnish

PREPARATION

1. In a bowl or pitcher, combine the cider, ginger beer, orange juice, cinnamon stick, and ice cubes.
2. Divide between glasses and garnish with sliced apples.

Pumpkin Juice

Pumpkin juice has always been a popular drink among the witches and wizards at Hogwarts. For breakfast, lunch, or dinner, this bubbly and refreshing drink is best served chilled but can also be served warm if the weather is particularly frosty.

SERVINGS: 3–4 ✦ PREPARATION TIME: 5 MINS

✳ INGREDIENTS

4 cups sparkling apple cider
½ cup pumpkin puree
2 teaspoons pumpkin pie spice
½ teaspoon vanilla extract
ice cubes
cinnamon sticks, to garnish

✳ PREPARATION

1. In a pitcher, stir together the cider, pumpkin puree, pumpkin pie spice, vanilla, and ice cubes until chilled and the spices are incorporated.
2. Pour into chilled glasses and garnish with a cinnamon stick.

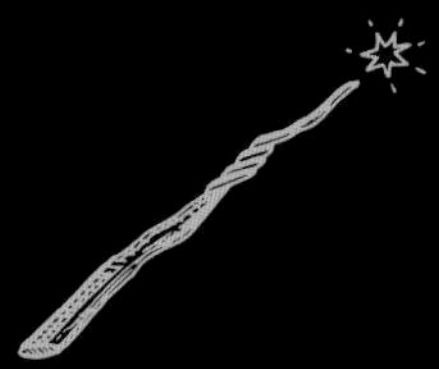

Headmistress's Afternoon Brew

Professor Umbridge is a cruel and brutal headmistress during her time at Hogwarts School of Witchcraft and Wizardry. It is quite a contrast from the bright pink and flowery ensembles she is known for. This bright pink drink is just perfect when you've had a long day of disciplining students.

SERVINGS: 2 ✦ PREPARATION TIME: 8 MINS

INGREDIENTS

- 2 ½ cups boiling water
- 8 to 10 pieces young rosebud tea
- 2 tablespoons prickly pear cactus powder
- 2 tablespoons simple syrup
- ½ cup heavy cream
- 1 tablespoon powdered sugar

PREPARATION

1. In a pot, pour the boiling water over the rosebud tea and let steep for 5 minutes.
2. Strain and stir in the cactus powder and simple syrup.
3. Whip the heavy cream with a hand mixer. Once frothy, add the powdered sugar and whip until soft peaks form.
4. Pour the tea into two cups and top with the lightly whipped cream. Stir and enjoy your afternoon brew.

Poison Apple Martini from Bella Notte

During Robert and Giselle's dinner at Bella Notte, the waiter presents a very special apple martini for Giselle to enjoy. Unable to resist, she raises the glass to her lips when Pip flies through the air and knocks the poisonous drink right out of her hands. This sweet and sour apple drink is vibrantly green to match the wicked intentions of Queen Narissa.

SERVINGS: 1 ✦ PREPARATION TIME: 5 MINS

✶ INGREDIENTS

1 ½ ounces sour apple schnapps
1 ½ ounces vodka
1 ounce apple cider
½ ounce lemon juice
½ ounce simple syrup
1 cup ice cubes
green apple slice, to garnish

✶ PREPARATION

1. **Combine the sour apple schnapps, vodka, apple cider, lemon juice, syrup, and ice in a cocktail shaker. Shake until cold.**
2. **Strain into a chilled glass and garnish with a slice of apple.**

MIDNIGHT MARGARITAS

"EYE OF NEWT AND TOE OF FROG, WOOL OF BAT AND TONGUE OF DOG, adder's fork and blindworm's sting, Barbados lime is just the thing. Cragged salt like a sailor's stubble, flip the switch and let the cauldron bubble!" Get your Midnight Margaritas bubbling over with this delicious cocktail recipe!

SERVINGS: 2 ✦ PREPARATION TIME: 10 MINS

INGREDIENTS

MARGARITA

lime wedges, for the rim
kosher salt, for the rim
3 ounces tequila
2 ounces triple sec
3 ounces lime juice
1 ounce jalapeño simple syrup
2 cups ice cubes

JALAPEÑO SIMPLE SYRUP

½ cup sugar
½ cup water
1 medium jalapeño, sliced

PREPARATION

1. To make the jalapeño simple syrup: In a saucepan over medium heat, combine the sugar and water. Bring the mixture to a boil and add the sliced jalapeños. Remove from the heat and let cool to room temperature. Strain out the jalapeños and reserve the simple syrup in a bottle or jar.
2. To make the margarita: Run a wedge of lime along the rims of two serving glasses and dip in salt to coat the rims.
3. Place the tequila, triple sec, lime juice, simple syrup, and ice in a blender and blend on high speed until smooth. Pour into the prepared glasses and enjoy as you dance around the kitchen.

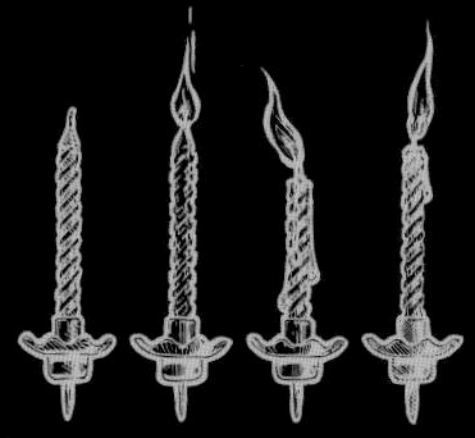

Sabrina's Purification Drink

ON SABRINA'S SIXTEENTH BIRTHDAY, she says goodbye to her mortal life and friends to attend er Dark Baptism and sign her name in the Book of the Beast. To prepare for the big event, Aunt ilda concocts a purification drink to help purify the temple of her body and cleanse Sabrina of ny toxins she may have. The frozen bananas provide a natural creamy sweetness to help carry the avors and benefits of mint and ginger.

SERVINGS: 2 ✦ **PREPARATION TIME: 5 MINS**

INGREDIENTS

- 2 cups baby spinach leaves, washed and dried
- 5 mint leaves
- 2 tablespoons lemon juice
- 1 frozen banana, sliced
- 1 cup milk of choice
- 1-inch piece fresh ginger, peeled and sliced
- 1 tablespoons spirulina powder

PREPARATION

1. **Combine the ingredients in a blender and blend on medium speed until smooth. Adjust the consistency with a bit of water. Serve in glasses and drink to purify the temple of your body.**

Life Potion

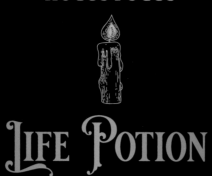

After returning to Salem on Halloween night three hundred years later, the Sanderson sisters retrieve their spell book and concoct the Life Potion, a bright green elixir meant to suck the youth out of all the children in town. The sisters' efforts are crushed when the potion is smashed to the ground. This tantalizing sweet and citrusy drink is the ultimate pick-me-up especially for the sisters when Halloween night doesn't play out as they hoped.

SERVINGS: 1 ✦ PREPARATION TIME: 5 MINS

INGREDIENTS

2 ounces Midori liqueur
1 ounce vodka
½ ounce lemon juice
½ ounce lime juice
2 ounces club or lemon and lime soda
ice cubes
dry ice (optional)
lime wedge, to garnish

PREPARATION

1. Fill a cocktail shaker with the Midori, vodka, lemon and lime juices, club soda, and ice. Shake until chilled, then strain into a chilled serving glass.
2. For an extra effect, add dry ice and garnish with a lime wedge.

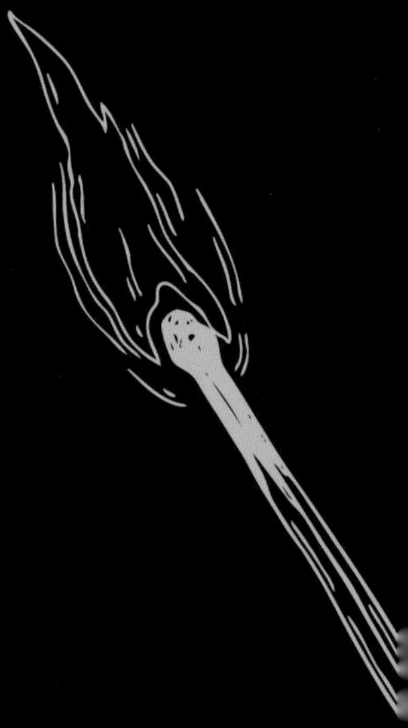

Bloody Mary

On the road to visit Whitmore College where Grams used to teach, Bonnie and Damon receive a crash course on how to handle Elena, a newly turned vampire. The three enter a frat party, with Bloody Marys in hand, to find that their methods of helping her are quite different.

SERVINGS: 1 ✦ PREPARATION TIME: 5 MINS ✦ COOKING TIME: 5 MINS

INGREDIENTS

1 lime wedge, for the rim
Old Bay Seasoning, for the rim
4 ounces tomato juice
2 ounces vodka
1 teaspoon horseradish
2 dashes Worcestershire sauce
1 or 2 dashes Tabasco hot sauce
⅛ teaspoon celery salt
½ ounce lime juice
ice cubes

GARNISHES
1 celery stick
1 cooked thick-cut bacon strip
3 stuffed green olives

PREPARATION

1. Run a lime wedge along the rim of your serving glass. Dip the rim in Old Bay Seasoning to coat and set aside.
2. Fill a cocktail shaker with the tomato juice, vodka, horseradish, Worcestershire sauce, Tabasco, celery salt, lime juice, and ice. Shake until chilled, then strain into the prepared glass.
3. Garnish with the celery, bacon, and olives.

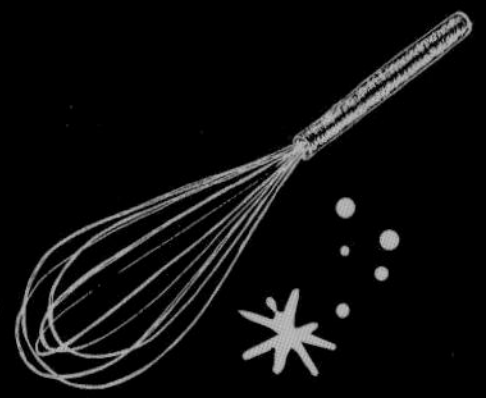

Agatha All Along

AGNES STARTS OFF AS THE TYPICAL NOSY NEIGHBOR TO WANDA AND VISION in the idyllic neighborhood of Westview. Unbeknownst to Wanda, Agnes is actually Agatha Harkness, one of the most powerful Salem witches, who thoroughly enjoys interfering with the sacred world Wanda has created. This drink appears just as dark and cynical as Agatha's magic. With the addition of lime juice, the drink will begin to turn purple right before your eyes to create a sweet and fizzy drink.

SERVINGS: 2 ✦ PREPARATION TIME: 5 MINS ✦ COOKING TIME: 5 MINS

INGREDIENTS

¼ cup butterfly pea flower
2 cups hot water
2 to 3 tablespoons simple syrup
ice cubes
¼ cup fresh lime juice
4 fresh blackberries
2 cups club soda

PREPARATION

1. In a mug, steep the butterfly pea flower in the hot water for 5 minutes. Strain and stir in the simple syrup to taste.
2. Pour the tea into chilled glasses with ice and stir half the lime juice into each. Top off each glass with club soda and garnish with the blackberries.

The Green Elixir

IT IS RUMORED THAT THE REASON FOR ELPHABA'S EMERALD GREEN SKIN is because of a green elixir her mother was given long ago from a visitor in Oz. Elphaba always keeps the bottle as a reminder of the explanation for her appearance. Glinda discovers this magical concoction and realizes who Elphaba's father really is.

SERVINGS: 2 ✦ PREPARATION TIME: 5 MINS ✦ COOKING TIME: 5 MINS

INGREDIENTS

1 ½ cups coconut milk
2 tablespoons emerald pandan powder
2 tablespoons simple syrup, or to taste
¼ teaspoon mint extract
ice cubes

PREPARATION

1. In a saucepan over medium heat, combine the coconut milk and pandan powder and bring just to a simmer. Remove from the heat and add the simple syrup.
2. Stir in the mint extract and pour over ice to serve.

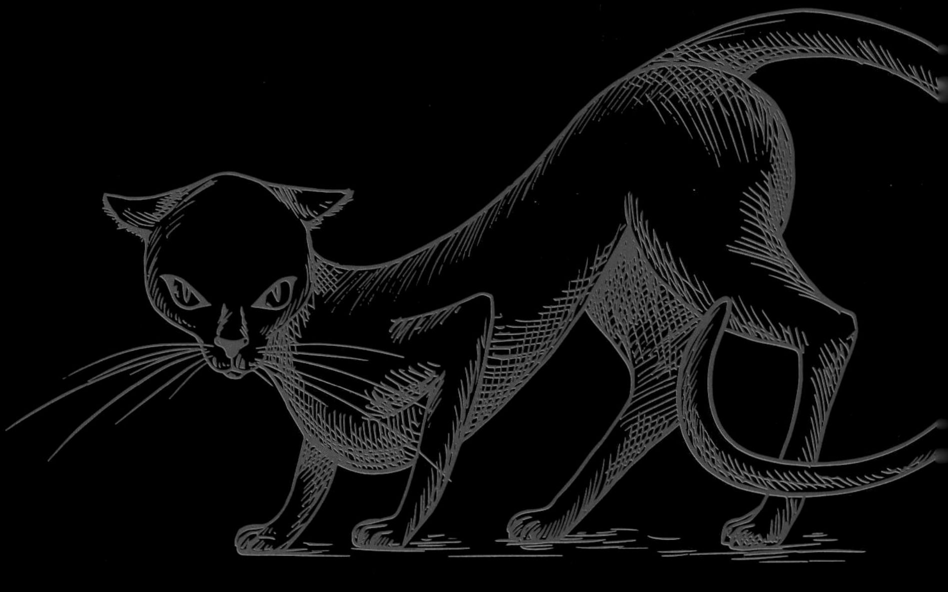

METRIC AND IMPERIAL CONVERSIONS

(These conversions are rounded for convenience)

INGREDIENT	CUPS/TABLESPOONS/ TEASPOONS	OUNCES	GRAMS/MILLILITERS
Salt	1 teaspoon	0.2 ounce	6 grams
Spices: cinnamon, cloves, ginger, or nutmeg (ground)	1 teaspoon	0.2 ounce	5 milliliters
Sugar, brown, firmly packed	1 cup	7 ounces	200 grams
Butter	1 cup/16 tablespoons/2 sticks	8 ounces	230 grams
Cheese, shredded	1 cup	4 ounces	110 grams
Cornstarch	1 tablespoon	0.3 ounce	8 grams
Cream cheese	1 tablespoon	0.5 ounce	14.5 grams
Flour, all-purpose	1 cup/1 tablespoon	4.5 ounces/0.3 ounce	125 grams/8 grams
Flour, whole wheat	1 cup	4 ounces	120 grams
Fruit, dried	1 cup	4 ounces	120 grams
Fruits or veggies, chopped	1 cup	5 to 7 ounces	145 to 200 grams
Fruits or veggies, pureed	1 cup	8.5 ounces	245 grams
Honey, maple syrup, or corn syrup	1 tablespoon	0.75 ounce	20 grams
Liquids: cream, milk, water, or juice	1 cup	8 fluid ounces	240 milliliters
Oats	1 cup	5.5 ounces	150 grams
Sugar, white	1 cup/1 tablespoon	7 ounces/0.5 ounce	200 grams/12.5 grams
Pure vanilla extract	1 teaspoon	0.2 ounce	4 grams

OVEN TEMPERATURES

FAHRENHEIT	CELSIUS	GAS MARK
225°	110°	¼
250°	120°	½
275°	140°	1
300°	150°	2
325°	160°	3

FAHRENHEIT	CELSIUS	GAS MARK
350°	180°	4
375°	190°	5
400°	200°	6
425°	220°	7
450°	230°	8

BIBLIOGRAPHY

WITCHES OF THE SCREEN AND STAGE

A Discovery of Witches: All Souls Trilogy, Deborah Harkness, Sky One, 2018.
Bewitched, William Asher, ABC, 1964.
Brave, Mark Andrews, Walt Disney Studios, 2012.
Buffy the Vampire Slayer, Joss Whedon, The WB, 1997.
Charmed, Constance M. Burge, The WB, 1998.
Chilling Adventures of Sabrina, Roberto Aguirre-Sacasa, Netflix, 2018
Enchanted, Kevin Lima, Walt Disney Studios, 2007.
Fantastic Beasts and Where to Find Them, David Yates, Warner Bros. 2016.
Hocus Pocus, Kenny Ortega, Walt Disney Pictures, 1993.
Kiki's Delivery Service, Takashi Shimizu, Toei Company Ltd., 2014.
Outlander, Donald R. Moore, Sony Pictures Television, 2014.
Practical Magic, Griffin Dunne, Warner Bros., 1998.
Snow White and the Seven Dwarfs, David Hand, Walt Disney Productions, 1938.
Spirited Away, Hayao Miyazaki, Toho, 2001.
Tangled, Nathan Greno, Walt Disney Studios Motion Pictures, 2010.
The Chronicles of Narnia, Andrew Adamson, Walt Disney Studios, 2005.
The Little Mermaid, John Musker, Walt Disney Pictures, 1989.
The Originals, Julie Plec, The CW, 2013.
The Vampire Diaries, Kevin Williamson, The CW, 2009.
The Witches, Nicolas Roeg, Warner Bros., 1990.
WandaVision, Jac Schaeffer, Marvel Studios, 2012.
Wicked, Winnie Holzman and Stephen Schwartz, 2003.

WITCHES OF LITERATURE

Aguirre-Sacasa, Roberto; *Chilling Adventures of Sabrina*, Archie Horror, 2014.
Arden, Katherine, *Winternight Trilogy: Bear and the Nightingale*, Del Rey, 2017.
Arden, Katherine, *Winternight Trilogy: The Girl in the Tower*, Del Rey, 2017.
Arden, Katherine, *Winternight Trilogy: The Winter of the Witch*, Del Rey, 2019.
Dahl, Roald, The Witches, Jonathan Cape, 1983.
Gabaldon, Diana, *Outlander*, Delacorte Books, 1991.
Harkness, Deborah, *A Discovery of Witches: All Souls Trilogy*, Penguin Books, 2011
Kadono, Eiko, *Kiki's Delivery Service*, Fukuinkan Shoten, 1985.
Maas, Sarah J., *Throne of Glass*, Bloomsbury Publishing, 2012-2018.
Maguire, Gregory, *Wicked*, ReganBooks, 1999.
Miller, Madeline, *Circe*, Little, Brown and Company, 2018.
Rowling, J.K., *Harry Potter and the Sorcerer's Stone*, Bloomsbury, 1997.
Rowling, J.K., *Harry Potter and the Chamber of Secrets*, Bloomsbury, 1998.
Rowling, J.K., *Harry Potter and the Prisoner of Azkaban*, Bloomsbury, 1999.
Rowling, J.K., *Harry Potter and the Goblet of Fire*, Bloomsbury, 2000.
Rowling, J.K., *Harry Potter and the Order of the Phoenix*, Bloomsbury, 2003.
Rowling, J.K., *Harry Potter and the Half-Blood Prince*, Bloomsbury, 2005.
Rowling, J.K., *Harry Potter and the Deathly Hallows*, Bloomsbury, 2007.
Smith, L.J., *The Vampire Diaries*, Harper Paperbacks, 1991.
Wynne Jones, Diana, *Howl's Moving Castle*, Greenwillow Books, 1986.

INDEX

R

S

T

V

About the Author

Deanna Huey grew up in San Francisco cooking in the small kitchen of her grandmother's apartment. At a very young age, she was always determined to create dishes her friends and family would love. The process of cooking and being in the kitchen was always a place of comfort and endless creativity. She started her professional culinary career working in fine dining restaurants and bakeries around the city. She now has expanded her culinary journey on her blog, *Feast of Starlight*, where she shares her love of stories and movies with food through recipes and photography.